FOUNDATIONS OF LAW IN A BUSINESS SOCIETY SERIES

LEGAL
HISTORY

LAW and SOCIAL CHANGE

Frederick G. Kempin, Jr.

**THE WHARTON SCHOOL OF
FINANCE AND COMMERCE
UNIVERSITY OF PENNSYLVANIA**

PRENTICE-HALL, INC.   ENGLEWOOD CLIFFS, NEW JERSEY

FOUNDATIONS OF LAW IN A BUSINESS SOCIETY SERIES

Library of Congress
Catalog Card No.: 63-19697
C

PRENTICE-HALL INTERNATIONAL, INC., *London*
PRENTICE-HALL OF AUSTRALIA, PTY., LTD., *Sydney*
PRENTICE-HALL OF CANADA, LTD., *Toronto*
PRENTICE-HALL FRANCE, S.A.R.L., *Paris*
PRENTICE-HALL OF INDIA PRIVATE LIMITED, *New Delhi*
PRENTICE-HALL OF JAPAN, INC., *Tokyo*
PRENTICE-HALL DE MEXICO, S.A., *Mexico City*

FOUNDATIONS OF LAW IN A BUSINESS SOCIETY

The nonprofessional study of law as a basic element in both liberal and business or technical education is today the subject of keen interest and a focal point of widening intellectual horizons. The fact that our legal institutions open avenues to the deeper understanding of our culture, our history, our polity and our economy is increasingly appreciated, while it remains generally accepted that basic analysis of the methods and substance of the common law is an essential element in technical training for business.

The Foundations of Law in a Business Society Series offers a "one-foot shelf" of short, convenient, inexpensive and authoritative books written by scholars eminent in their respective fields, systematically covering the subjects of primary interest to all nonprofessional students of the law—both in the liberal and in the technical fields. Many of the titles will be useful also to law students, professional administrators, and general readers.

From the teacher's viewpoint, the essence of the Series is flexibility and freedom of choice. No longer must courses be built around the limited content or restricted approach of a single text. No longer must subjects be presented in fixed order. No longer must the experimentally-minded teacher struggle to develop course materials from scattered sources. Now it is practical and convenient to offer a course specifically designed for given interests and aptitudes without loss of the unity and scope of a conventional textbook.

Various teaching methods and conceptual orientations are provided for. Both text and case materials are included, and the latest doctrinal developments and statutory codifications are fully reflected in the several titles, each of which is complete in itself yet an integral part of a carefully-planned structure.

The Foundations of Law in a Business Society Series covers the legal process, the history and philosophy of law, and the major areas of public and private law, emphasizing always the role of law in contemporary society and mankind's eternal quest for justice.

Cornelius W. Gillam

PREFACE

This book is about the history of Anglo-American law. It assumes that the reader is only casually acquainted with either English history or the law. It tells a continued story of the development of the institutions of the law—its courts, juries, judges, and lawyers—and traces the beginnings and development of selected legal concepts such as property in land, contract, liability for injury, negotiability of commercial paper, and the business corporation.

A knowledge of legal history is essential in three areas: first, as a part of general cultural history, for law is a significant part of all cultures; second, as a necessary tool in the understanding, criticism, and assessment of the current state of the law; third, as an integrating medium in the understanding of economic, social, and political history, for each of these affects, and is affected by, the law.

Legal history can dispel many commonly held illusions about the law. One of the most common of these illusions is that the law is held in the iron bands of tradition through the doctrine of precedent. Like most errors, this one is partly fact and partly fancy. While the law values experience more highly than logic, this grounding in reality is intended to promote desirable and orderly change, not to forestall it. Logic may presuppose unalterable truth. In the law, unalterable truth may take the form of a fixed and doctrinaire code, or the form of revealed principles of natural law. In giving second place to logic in the formulation of law, the common law denies the primacy of legal codes and hesitates to adopt the principles of natural law, not knowing who is capable of expounding them. The common law prefers to adopt as law the practical rules that experience has proved to be workable. Experience, however, is only a starting point for change. It is only one factor in the legal process. History, sociology, economics, politics, and natural-law philosophy—all have had their influence. Viewed in this way, the law's approach to its problems is not much different from the Anglo-American approach to social and economic problems in general. Rigid conformity with doctrine is alien to this society.

Two subsidiary errors stem from the basic error of overestimating conservatism of the law. The first, made by those who are suspicious of all change, is criticism of the law when it does change, on the ground that it should not. The other, a mistake made by those who desire radical change, is to criticize the law when it does not change, believing that it cannot. The first group would raise experience to the status of doctrine, an elevation leading to stagnant traditionalism. The second group would ignore our legal heritage and perhaps lead us to unworkable utopianism. The law chooses the middle path.

Precedent, experience, and tradition provide the basis for stability but are also the starting points for change. Successive cases provide opportunities for subtle changes in the meanings of words, unnoticed alterations of approaches to analysis, and minute developments of concepts. Sometimes gradually, sometimes suddenly, it will be realized that a new legal idea has come into being.

The history of the law is one of change. Without the need for violent social revolution, the common law has adapted to changes in our social and economic structure from feudalism through mercantilism and into a modern industrial capitalistic society. It has conquered royal absolutism. It has overcome domineering judges. It has absorbed the world of business and has kept the power of money within controllable limits.

Not all of this has been done by the judges. From time to time they have needed legislative prodding in order to respond to new conditions. The common law's balance between stability and change, tradition and experiment, was too much at times for courts to maintain. This, too, is a part of legal history.

The twentieth century is not the end of legal history. It is, however, as every century before it has been, a time for assessment and choice. In law, as in other areas of human activity and learning, three valid questions may be asked: where did it come from, where is it, and where is it going? Where law came from can be traced only through legal history; where it is, now, can be partly explained by legal history; where it is going is indicated by trends revealed in the study of legal history. It is the task of legal history to refresh the social recollection and to add criticism and analysis to basic historical information.

Frederick G. Kempin, Jr.

CONTENTS

PART I

The
Background
of the
Common Law

What legal history is about

THE LAW—AS WAS SAID WITH RESIGNATION of the poor—is always with us. Some twenty centuries before the Christian Era, Hammurabi promulgated his famous code for Babylonia; and the Mosaic code of the Israelites is only eight centuries younger. Even before those ancient codes, practices and customs were the equivalent of law, if not true law in the modern sense, among primitive people. Some primitive societies in our own day are still controlled by such amorphous law.

Every legal rule, idea, or norm had its own genesis. All started somewhere and had some cause. Some came about by chance, and thought gave birth to others. Some stemmed from one man's weakness; others were the fruit of strength. Some still echo with the noise of ancient struggles; while passing time and change of custom formed some others.

Today, as ever, law pervades our lives. This is its nature, because law guides our relations with each other. It tells us how we may be punished for our crimes; it makes us pay when, by our fault, we injure others; it says what we must do if we want our promises to be enforced as contracts; it makes us pay our taxes; it requires us to take out licenses in order to engage in business, to get married, and even to practice such a pastoral pastime as the art of angling.

Every mature system of law has a long history from its inception as a system, back through its archaic and almost forgotten predecessors, to its remote origin in its primitive-law background. Our Anglo-American system of law has been relatively mature (in the sense that it has been the object of study by a separate legal profession) for the past eight hundred years. It was preceded by the archaic and almost lost legal system of the Anglo-Saxons and finds its remote origins in the laws of the Germanic tribes which settled England in the middle of the first millennium.

Most modern Anglo-American legal concepts have been developed in the past eight hundred years. A few may stem from Anglo-Saxon times, but it would take considerable imagination to find precursors of modern law in the primitive Germanic system. On the other hand, our law has not been developed in isolation from the law of the rest of the Western world. No little debt is owed to Roman law, and the canon law of the Church has contributed its share of ideas.

A realistic point in time to begin a discussion of Anglo-American legal history, then, is with the common law as it stood when it first became the object of study by a distinct legal profession, though excursions into the time before, and into other systems, will be necessary to explain particular points. This initial date is the beginning of the thirteenth century.

What is meant by legal history

The history of law tells of the development of an important segment of human thought and of the social institutions based upon it. Human thought can be developed either individually or institutionally. Philosophical thought, for instance, is developed by those who work out their ideas in the light of their own experiences, knowledge, and insight. Philosophers build on the expressed opinions of prior thinkers by rejecting some ideas, altering others, and, sometimes, by adding new ones. Most legal thought, however, has been developed anonymously in the processes and procedures of the courtroom and the legislative chamber. It has been institutionally, not individually, developed.

Sometimes individual thought is adopted as a part of law. Political and, of recent years, economic thought are examples. Much of our current constitutional law was originally developed by individuals and then adopted by the framers or judicial interpreters of our constitutions. Our antitrust statutes recognize economic thinking. Legal philosophy, called jurisprudence, at times has found its way into judicial and legislative determinations. Jurisprudence in itself is not law; it is the thought of individuals about law and what the law should be.

Institutionally developed law is expressed through officially recognized agencies, such as the chief of a tribe in a primitive society, the king of a nation, a council of wise men, or a legislature. In our day and country the channels through which the law is made known are the state and federal legislatures, the courts, and the administrative agencies, in the form of statutes, decisions, and regulations.

The building blocks of legal history are the written records left by these official promulgators of the law. For times in which no records were kept, we must rely on statements of others concerning the nature of the law that controlled society. In the primitive stage of our law, the Germanic invaders of England kept no written records. Almost everything we know about their law has been left to us by those whom they conquered. When the tribes combined into larger kingdoms in England, written records began to appear. There are old collections of "dooms" of the Anglo-Saxon kings, which set forth penalties for "crimes." Ancient charters, literary works, and some traditions that were eventually put in writing have trickled through to tell us other things.

With the coming of the Normans, written records began to multiply. First came Domesday Book, in 1086, then the records of Glanvill in 1187, Bracton in 1256, and finally, the records of the courts themselves in the latter half of the 1200's. The stream of legal records broadened, and today it is a vast torrential river which threatens to engulf us.

By legal history, then, we mean the development of the concepts, doctrines, and rules which have been created and used to keep order in our society. They arose at particular times out of particular circumstances and, to the extent possible, should be examined in the light of those times and circumstances. Possibly the easiest error to make in the study of legal history is to assume that because an ancient and a modern doctrine, rule, or institution have the same or similar names, they are therefore identical. In their continuance and development, the substance of these doctrines often changed remarkably, and this, too, is the stuff of legal history.

The pre-Norman scene

The early thirteenth century lawyers whose efforts were to culminate in the creation of a new legal system, the common law, were the products of the Norman Conquest. Descendants of the Scandinavian conquerors of western France, the Normans were administrators. They brought little written law with them to England, but they transformed the existing Anglo-Saxon law. Their faculty for administration developed the Norman courts and legislative bodies whose processes created our earliest body of modern law.

The Norman conquerors of 1066 did not enter a virgin wilderness, and they did not conquer savages. They conquered a country with a fairly well-defined system of government, including law and courts of law. William the Conqueror purported to enter as legitimate occupant of the throne, and with that claim, he could not very easily have displaced existing Anglo-Saxon law had he so desired. In truth, the Normans had nothing much with which to displace it. Their law was not radically dissimilar in concept or in practice from Anglo-Saxon law. In administration, the Normans were far ahead of their English subjects; but in law, no such clear advantage existed.

The basic values of the conquered society were those common to all Germanic nations. The relationship between a vassal and his lord was primary. The follower owed his lord protection during life and the avengement of his wrongful death. A similar obligation made it necessary for a man to take vengeance or to obtain compensation when a member of his family was killed. The rules of such blood feuds were closely regulated by law and custom: in the type of vengeance that might be taken, in the amount of compensation that might be exacted, in the place at which the compensation should be paid, and in the circumstances under which compensation need not be paid. If a man was killed as a convicted thief, no vengeance could be taken by his kin, and the same exemption applied to one who killed another while defending his lord or a close female relative. The influence of the Church on the side of compensation instead of physical vengeance tended to temper the violence of the times, but the blood feud survived until after the Conquest, with varying degrees of strength, in all parts of England.

Pre-Norman government was decentralized. Shires (counties) had long been the basic units of government, some of them having been the domains of the Germanic conquerors who came five centuries before the Normans. A sheriff, an ealdorman, and the bishop governed the shires, with little assistance or hindrance from the royal government. There was, indeed, a king, but he usually governed in concert with a council of wise men called the witan, frequently convened by the weaker kings, and not at all by some of the stronger ones. In either case, the king's power was not great, and his kingship was not hereditary, since the witan had the right to elect his successor.

Each county was divided into administrative units called hundreds, roughly parallel to our townships or parishes, and responsible only to the county. The smallest units were the vills, settlements in which ordinary folk lived.

And last, there were the boroughs, large and small, usually fortified in Anglo-Saxon days. But when trade grew and modes of warfare demanded walled castles, boroughs became locations for fairs and markets.

Changes effected by the Normans

The Norman conquerors made certain changes in administration which, although they were to have radical effects, did not greatly alter existing English customs. Instead of the indeterminate Anglo-Saxon witan, composed of such important men as the king chose or felt compelled to call into assembly, the Normans created the Great Council, or Magna Curia. It was composed of the king, all the lords to whom he had given extensive tracts of land as a reward for their faithfulness, many English lords who chose to swear allegiance to him, and great ecclesiastics. Its composition, more certain than that of the witan, was not absolutely fixed. From it, the House of Lords ultimately emerged, and added to it was what became the House of Commons. These are obvious models for American bicameral legislatures.

The Norman kings obtained control of the shires or counties simply by appointing the county sheriffs. That office ceased to be hereditary and became subject to the close control of the king and his administrative officers in the Exchequer (financial office). The palatine counties in the north and west were exceptions because they were military buffers against the Welsh and Scots, and in return they were granted virtual independence. As part of a plan to set up separate Courts Christian for ecclesiastical matters, the bishop was removed from the administration of the county. The ealdorman, whose influence had declined before the Conquest, disappeared.

In administration, the Norman kings used personal confidants who were charged with specific duties, sometimes judicial, sometimes ambassadorial, sometimes purely administrative. These officials, who might perform many different types of tasks during their careers, constituted the lesser council, or household, and together with the great council were part of the King's Court, or Curia Regis.

In Anglo-Saxon times, a loose lord-vassal relationship had existed. A person who held a large tract of land had in his entourage a number of thanes who originally were warriors. Each thane was entrusted with a tract of land, usually not transferable to his heirs, from which, by using the labor of the villeins, he could support himself. The Normans, however, exchanged this for an adaptation of Continental feudalism. Feudalism was a system of landholding based on a personal relationship. In return for an oath of homage, the king granted vast tracts of land to privileged chief lords, on condition that certain services should perpetually be rendered to him. These lords could then grant portions of their land to other lesser lords, in return for an oath of homage or fealty, again on condition of perpetual services. The system was military in its inception, for the highest type of feudal relationship was based on the tenant's giving military service to his overlord.

Anglo-Saxon and early Norman law

Except for the written dooms of a few kings setting down penalties for crimes, Anglo-Saxon law was custom and custom was law. There was neither a legal profession nor any body of technical knowledge.

Because the law of crimes (if we can call it that) was written, we know something about it. The listed crimes were those of violence and disloyalty: treason, homicide, wounding, assault, rape, and theft. For treason, the punishment was death. For homicide, compensation might be paid unless it was accomplished by poison or from ambush. For a killing in an open fight, a sum (*bot*) was paid, part of which (the *wer*) went to the king, and the remainder (the *wite*) to the kin of the deceased. A scale of compensation for lesser injuries fixed a higher rate for important persons, churchmen, and nuns than for the general population. Theft, in Anglo-Saxon times, might result in slavery for not only the thief but his family. If caught in the act or fleeing with the loot, a thief could be killed.

Since there was little commerce, there was little commercial law. Its content is to some extent conjectural. Contract in the modern sense was unknown, and sales took place by delivery of the article sold; or if delivery was to be made in the future, it was secured by a deposit or by a pledge (*wed*) which would be forfeited for nondelivery. Promises under oath were not uncommon, and their breach put one within the jurisdiction of the Church.

There was little ownership of land as we know it, that is, in the form of an interest which can be sold or willed to one's heirs. Some lands given by a written charter from the king and witan might be devised by wills, but these were uncommon.

Preliminary definitions

The law, in common with other areas of learning, has specialized meanings for certain words and phrases. Since recurrent use will be made of some of these terms, the most usual of them will be explained, preliminarily, at this point.

The common law and the civil law. The term "common law" refers to the system of law developed in England and transferred to most of the English-speaking world. It is distinguished from the civil-law system used in Continental Europe and in those nations settled by European peoples. One or the other of the systems is the basis of law in most of the free world.

Many ancient systems of law, such as the Egyptian, Babylonian, and Greek, have totally disappeared. Others, such as the Hindu, Japanese, and Chinese, have been incorporated in some measure into modern systems. Of non-Western systems that survive, the Mohammedan is the most important: Islamic law is based on the Koran, as interpreted by tradition and juristic writings. As Islamic nations separate law from religion, however, non-Islamic models tend to be followed.

The civil-law system can be traced back to Roman law, which extended to the limits of the Empire. With the disintegration of Rome, its law lost its universality. Wherever it was applied, it received admixtures of local customs and differed in content in the various parts of Europe. Civil law received its modern impetus from the early nineteenth-century French codes of law created by French jurists under the direct leadership of Napoleon Bonaparte. The common law, however, is purely a product of English constitutional development.

The basic distinction between the two systems lies in the sources of law upon which they rely. The common-law system uses prior decided cases as very high sources of authority. The doctrine of *stare decisis* (let the decision stand) in one of its forms is the essence of the common-law system. That doctrine states that courts should adhere to the law as set forth in prior cases decided by the highest court of a given jurisdiction as long as the principle derived from those cases is logically essential to their decision, is reasonable, and is appropriate to contemporary circumstances. Different courts apply this general policy with varying degrees of strictness; English courts, for instance, are inclined to be more rigorous than American courts in its application.

The civil law, on the other hand, is oriented toward a legislative code of laws, a comprehensive enactment of all the basic law of the country. When a controversy is presented to a court or lawyer, the immediate problem is to find the appropriate code provision covering the situation and then to apply it to the problem at hand. The courts look to the writings of scholars to aid them in interpreting code provisions. Cases are not ignored, but they do not have anything approaching binding authority on judges.

Statutes in common-law jurisdictions. Common-law jurisdictions, of course, rely on statutes as well as on court decisions. The modern trend is to enlarge the role of statutes, so that they cover a large proportion of legal problems. Some of the United States even compile their statutes into what are called codes. In addition, particular segments of the law are "codified" in all jurisdictions, so that there are criminal codes, negotiable instruments statutes, sales statutes, and, lately, the Uniform Commercial Code, which covers a broad spectrum of commercial law.

The common-law courts have, in common with civil-law courts, the right to interpret statutes, but the rules of statutory interpretation are many and difficult to apply. In the United States the general policy is to attempt to interpret a statute in the light of the intention of the legislature. In England, on the other hand, courts have often held that a statute should be read without reference to legislative intent.

Constitutionality. The courts of the United States, together with those of West Germany and Australia, can go one step further. They can declare a statute to be invalid because it conflicts with their written constitutions. This is true not only of the Supreme Court and lower federal courts of the United States, which can declare both state and federal statutes void for contravention of the Constitution of the United States, but also of state courts, which can declare state statutes void for contravention of the state or federal constitutions.

Judicial review of legislation is foreign to most civil-law countries. Consequently, the legislatures make the ultimate decision as to the constitutional propriety of legislation. West Germany is a notable exception, and Brazil, Burma, and Japan have a degree of judicial review. France, since 1958, has had a Constitutional Council with some power in that connection, but the council is not part of the French judicial system.

England has no written constitution, but its form of government under an amalgam of customs and ancient statutes, which are its "unwritten" constitution, is as definite and as certain as our own. The pivot of English government is the cabinet system, which is purely customary and does not depend on statutory authority. Restraints upon government are essential elements of English government, and that part of our written constitution which we call the Bill of Rights is, in most of its particulars, no less firmly entrenched in English law than in our own.

It appears to be the opinion of the English courts that no court in England may declare a statute void on the ground that it is unconstitutional. This does not keep English courts from exercising control over statutes, however. Through the device of interpretation, for instance, any court, whether in the civil- or the common-law system, can keep statutes in line with generally accepted principles and can even, on occasion, entirely emasculate a statute.

Civil law distinguished from criminal law.   Within a legal system the term "civil law" is used to distinguish private actions from public wrongs, which fall under the heading of criminal law. When one person, organization, corporation, or branch of government sues another in order to obtain a remedy for a supposed injury, the case is a civil case, leading to a possible remedy in money damages or an order to do or not to do a certain act. When the state prosecutes an individual or corporation for breach of a rule of conduct set up by the legislature, the case is a criminal case, which may result in a fine or imprisonment.

The same transaction may give rise to both a civil and a criminal action. A simple case of assault and battery, for instance, may result in a civil action by the victim to obtain damages for injuries sustained and also in a criminal action by the state to punish the guilty party by fine or imprisonment.

Common law and equity.   The term "common law" is also used to distinguish one segment of Anglo-American law from another part called equity. Today the terms refer to different sets of legal doctrines. In a very few states these different legal doctrines are applied by separate and distinct courts.

For centuries the English legal system had two types of courts existing side by side. The older of the two was known as the common-law courts. Another set of courts, including the Courts of Chancery and Star Chamber, developed those principles we now call equitable.

Basically, the courts applying equitable principles acted when the common-law courts either would not act or reached results that were too strict and technical and therefore unjust. The net result of their activities was the creation of a set of principles to be applied when the common law did not provide a suitable remedy for a particular wrong. It is still basic theory that one cannot obtain an equitable remedy if an adequate legal remedy is available.

Definition of a court.   The word "court" has been used in many senses. It derives from the Latin word *curia* and was originally used to refer to the rectangular enclosed yard of a medieval house. It came to refer to a group of persons either formally or informally gathered together, and so we speak, for instance, of a reception at the Queen's Court. The early English royal councils were referred to as *curiae* or courts. Since the earliest justices were members of the King's Council, they were part of his court. This meaning of the word as an assembly of persons is still used in Massachusetts, where the legislature is called the General Court. The early English law courts, composed of a number of "suitors," were called courts because they were groups of persons. When a single judge came to preside over the proceedings, the word "court" was applied to him or to the place at which he presided. When the office of judge became separated from the King's Council and attained a position of constitutional independence, the term continued in use.

Trial and appellate courts.   Every modern court system has both trial and appellate courts. The trial courts are courts of first instance and have two functions: to determine the facts and to apply the applicable law to those facts. Appellate courts, on the other hand, have only one function: to determine whether the trial court applied the correct law.

A trial court consists, usually, of one judge who presides over the trial and rules on questions including the adequacy of the lawyers' written pleadings, the admissibility of evidence, and the law in the case. If there is a jury, it decides what the facts were, on the basis of the evidence presented, and usually applies the law to those facts in accordance with the judge's charge. If there is no jury, the judge both decides the facts and applies the law.

An appellate court consists of three or more judges. If it finds that the trial court erred, it may, in appropriate circumstances, either grant a new trial or reverse the trial court's verdict without a new trial. For instance, if it believes the trial judge erroneously admitted or excluded testimony or incorrectly charged the jury, it may order a new trial. If there was no jury and if there is no question about the judge's conclusion of facts or about the admissibility of evidence, but only the question of whether the judge of the trial court applied the correct law, the appellate court may simply reverse the lower court and grant judgment for the other party.

The courts

SINCE THE LAW DEVELOPED IN THE PROC-
esses of the courts and legislatures, with the assistance
of the legal profession, we must carefully examine the
origins and processes of these institutions. The form
of an organization and the substance of its activities
are indissolubly intertwined. What, for instance,
would become of baseball if there were only two
bases? We might have cricket. Or what would become of corporate management if proxies were once
again made illegal? How would congressional com-
mittees perform if seniority were removed as a basis
for chairmanship? How many Supreme Court decisions on constitutional issues would stand if Congress,
by statute, could overrule them? This interrelationship
of form and substance gives primary importance to
a discussion of the emergence of courts, juries, and
the legal profession. In many cases, the way the law
developed was closely affected by the organizational
structure of those institutions at the time the concept,
doctrine, or rule had its origin.

Today we say that the judge determines the law;
this has been true for the past seven hundred years.
But until long after the Conquest, judges were unknown. There were "courts," but they were composed of lay persons called suitors, who answered
questions of "law" on the basis of their knowledge
of local customs. The heads of these bodies—the reeves,
sheriffs, lords, and stewards—merely presided. Law
was not yet a specialized body of knowledge that
needed professional judges.

Before royal justice dispensing a common law could come into being (i.e., a law uniform throughout the kingdom), it had to displace the existing system of courts. These courts, at the time of the Conquest, were the communal courts of the shire and hundred, the seignorial courts, and the borough courts.

Hundred and shire courts. Composed of lay suitors, the hundred court was presided over by the hundred reeve, the shire court by the shire reeve, or sheriff. After the Conquest, the hundred court lost its jurisdiction over cases involving land and whatever jurisdiction it may have had over criminal cases, but retained the remainder of its civil jurisdiction. At large semiannual meetings of the hundred, the sheriff of the county would take Pleas of the Crown, crimes reported by the reeve and four men of each vill, accompanied by the delivery of the suspects. Some of the offenders were amerced (fined) on the spot, and those accused of more grievous offenses were held for trial at the shire court.

Although there was no appeal from the hundred to the shire court, the shire court was the more important, because it covered a larger territory encompassing numerous hundreds and because its suitors and litigants were the most important persons in the county. In both courts the finding of the suitors was final unless they were guilty of prejudice or of improper procedure. In such cases, resort could theoretically be had to the king and his Council directly.

With the move toward administrative centralization after the Norman Conquest, the shires lost power. Not only was the sheriff made, in most instances, the king's man, but the most important cases were removed from the county court to the royal councils. First to meet that fate were those criminal cases known as Pleas of the Crown and, beginning a century after the Conquest, cases involving the most important form of wealth of those days—land.

Finally, in the thirteenth century, county courts were restricted to cases involving no more than forty shillings. The inexorable reduction in the value of money over the centuries meant that ultimately only the smallest claims could be heard in the shire courts. Inflation, together with the thirteenth century rule that suitors could send agents in their places, reduced the prestige of the county courts and increased, in turn, the importance of royal justice.

Seignorial courts. Not so ancient as the communal courts, but in existence at the time of the Conquest, were the seignorial courts, based on the concept that lords had the right and duty to hold court for their underlings.

Under the form of feudalism introduced by William the Conqueror, each royal grantee of land could grant portions of it to junior tenant lords, and so on down the feudal ladder to the lord who ultimately, through his villeins, worked the land. This process was known as subinfeudation. One who granted land to another was known as the tenant in service, because he did not actually use the land but was only entitled to services from his own tenant. The one who ultimately worked the land, through his villeins, was known as the tenant in demesne.

Each tenant in service had the right and duty to hold court for his junior tenants. This court, composed of all the tenants, decided their disputes and could be asked to advise the lord on problems of mutual concern. The greatest of the seignorial courts was the court of the king, who was at the top of the feudal pyramid. It was known as the Curia Regis. Courts in the intermediate rungs of the feudal ladder were known as Honors, or Courts Baron, and in these courts a tenant in chief (one who held his land directly under the king), for example, would meet with the barons who held land under him to obtain their advice and preside over the resolution of their disputes.

Lords who had purchased hundreds from the king had the right to hold the hundred court and to take the profits inevitably produced. In some of these courts, known as Courts Leet, even the sheriff was excluded from making his tourn (i.e., a semiannual visit to hold court on circuit).

The manorial court for the tenants or villeins on the land was the court of the tenant in demesne. Courts for villeins had the lord or his steward for a judge; those with jurisdiction over freemen, however, had the lord or his steward for presiding officer and freeman for suitors.

The powers of manorial courts varied according to the customs of the manor. Some had the right to fix prices of basic commodities made and sold on the manor—an important right, since the manor was a relatively self-sufficient economic unit, producing its own food and clothing. All could try civil actions between tenants or villeins, and had some criminal jurisdiction, although this latter varied in extent from manor to manor. Some, for instance, had the right to hang a thief caught within the manor; others could hang a thief no matter where he might have been caught.

The administrative functions of manorial courts, which included the allocation of services to be rendered to the lord by the various tenants, continued well into the eighteenth century, and records of copyhold estates in land were kept on the manors until 1925, when an act of Parliament modernized the law.

Borough courts. The boroughs had their own courts in which the citizens of the boroughs, the burgesses, were the suitors. These courts did not have criminal jurisdiction, for that was in the hands of the king. If a person within a borough owned land under a lord, he also owed suit to the court of that lord.

The boroughs as centers of trade and commerce were particularly adept in branches of the law involving those activities. The royal law, when it finally came into being, was intended primarily for a landed aristocracy concerned mainly with problems of real estate; the borough law might be said to have reflected bourgeois problems. Borough courts were in part responsible for the development of commercial law, since many of the disputes that came before them involved merchants and artisans.

Borough courts resisted encroachments of royal jurisdiction for centuries and were still a potent force at the time the American colonies were founded. Indeed, some authorities maintain that borough law was the law most familiar to many of our influential early settlers, and that early American law contained a heavy admixture of borough law.

Beginnings of the royal courts

The king's Magna Curia, or Great Council, was the most majestic of English courts. It consisted of all the tenants in chief, other magnates, and great ecclesiastics whom the king might call to attend. The king's personal advisers also met with it. This Great Council performed a multitude of duties, which were not separated into the modern classifications of executive, legislative, and judicial. It advised the king on matters of state, decided cases between the tenants in chief, accomplished accords between Church and state, and acted as a legislature.

The king's personal advisers, meeting alone, constituted another distinct court known as the Lesser Curia, or Household. From the members of this body the king chose justices to take care of his affairs throughout the realm, including the dispensing of justice, particularly criminal justice. The king's justices were particularly important in the close supervision of the shires. They saw to the collection of taxes by the sheriffs, to the punishment of those who were guilty of offenses included within the ever-expanding list of Pleas of the Crown, and they superseded the sheriff as presiding officers over the shire courts when they made their rounds. It should not be forgotten that for almost four hundred years after the Conquest, the king of England was also duke of large areas of France, and his justices journeyed there as well.

With the passage of time, additional specialized duties were given these personal representatives of the king. There were Justices of Gaol Delivery, who tried smaller criminal cases; traveling Commissioners of Oyer and Terminer (to hear and decide) who decided important criminal cases, and, until the fourteenth century, the General Eyre of the Justices in Eyre, who made penetrating investigations into all aspects of shire administration.

From 1195 onward, the Crown appointed local citizens to aid in the administration of justice. They were organized by the Statute of Winchester (1285) and, in general, had the duty of keeping custody of indicted prisoners until the king's justices arrived to try them. Permanent appointment commenced in 1327. In 1344, in conjunction with other persons in the county who were "learned in the law," they were given the power to try prisoners for felonies and breaches of the peace. In 1368 they were empowered to try some prisoners by themselves. It was around this time that they acquired the title of justice of the peace.

Reforms of Henry II and origins of central courts

In the reign of Henry II (1154-1189) there began a series of events which ultimately resulted in a system of royal courts and a law common to all of England. The movement started with an implementation of the royal claim to ownership of all the land in England.

The king's court had always had power to decide land cases involving tenants in chief who held directly of the Crown. Disputes between lesser lords were decided in the court of the lord of whom the land was held and who was tenant in service over it. Early in the twelfth century the king began to interfere with this jurisdiction by a decree stating that the lord's court could hear a case involving important interests in land only if a writ of right had been directed to him by the king. This writ, or letter, from the king directed the lord to do justice between the plaintiff who demanded the land and the defendant in possession, and stated that if this were not done the king would hear the case (indeed, he usually did). Later, on the fiction that the lord had surrendered to the king his right to hold court, the writ was issued directly to the defendant, thus bypassing the lord's court and bringing land cases directly into the royal courts.

The involved nature of the proceedings under this writ, the delays that could be interposed, the primitive mode of proof, and the fact that the decision could be contested by third parties if they acted within a year and a day—all this made the writ of right something less than an ideal remedy.

In 1166 Henry II devised the first of a new series of writs called the possessory assizes and designed to remedy the defects in the writ of right. The first writ, called *Novel Disseisin,* directed the sheriff of the county in which the land lay to gather twelve men of the neighborhood to determine whether the person on the land had, in fact, wrongfully taken it from the plaintiff, as alleged. The issue raised was dispossession, not ownership. If it was determined that the defendant had dispossessed the plaintiff, he was required to return the land, and if he still claimed to be the true owner, he, in turn, had to bring a writ of right. This procedure finally disposed of most cases.

The Court of Common Pleas.   The possessory assizes proved so popular that the King's Council could not take care of all the cases brought. In 1178 five justices were appointed from the king's retinue to hear them. These justices were subservient to the Council and reported to it, but their position differed from that of other king's justices in that they had a continuing commission and did not operate on an *ad hoc* basis. At first they devoted their attention exclusively to the hearing of civil cases involving land. Their conclusions were reported in Council, and in theory the Council made the actual decision.

The procedure initiated at this time was critical in the history of the common law. The "bench," as this group of justices was called for a short time, did not hear cases on application of the litigants directly. The litigants had first to purchase a writ, or letter, from the office of the chancellor, who issued writs only for types of cases authorized by the Council, of which he was a member. Only a limited number of these writs were authorized by the Council, and this number could be increased only gradually, for each addition to the register of writs constituted an infringement on the jurisdiction of the older communal and seignorial courts.

In the century following 1178, the bench gradually freed itself of subservience to the Council. In 1234 it started to keep its own records, and in 1272 it was given a chief justice. After Magna Carta (1215) its location was fixed at Westminster. In the third decade of the thirteenth century it acquired its final name, the Court of Common Pleas.

In addition to its jurisdiction over land cases, the Common Pleas soon acquired jurisdiction over other civil disputes such as actions to enforce obligations under a sealed instrument by the writ of covenant and actions to enforce payment of the agreed price of goods sold and delivered by the writ of debt. The court, of course, could not invent these writs, as they were issued by the chancellor on the authority of the Council.

The Court of King's Bench. Cases other than those for which writs were authorized by the Council were still heard by the King in Council. For instance, those important criminal matters called Pleas of the Crown were still in his hands. These too, however, were delegated to permanent bodies as they became more numerous and time-consuming.

The body to which criminal cases were delegated was called, in its full name, "The Justices Assigned for the holding of Pleas before the King Himself." Its common name is King's Bench. In theory the king, but actually the assigned justices, decided its cases. This court was so much a part of the King's Council that noble members of the Council attended some of its sessions. By the reign of Edward I (1272-1307) it was sufficiently disengaged from the Council to be recognized as a separate court.

This court exercised power over the king's other officials through the writ *quo warranto*, which asked "by what authority" they held a certain office or did a certain act. Power over other courts was exercised by writs of prohibition, mandamus, and certiorari. Writs of prohibition ordered another court to cease its consideration of a case. A writ of mandamus orders a public official or body to perform an act or restore a privilege. The writ of certiorari orders another court to send up its record for review. Writs of error and bills of exception were developed for the purpose of reviewing Common Pleas errors on the record.

The power of King's Bench to review cases decided in Common Pleas derived from the fact that Common Pleas decisions had been subject to review by the full Council at the time when King's Bench was still an integral part of it. When judicial duties were delegated to King's Bench, the power to review Common Pleas decisions was among them; and when King's Bench finally separated fully from the Council, this jurisdiction continued. The errors reviewed were primarily technical or procedural, and the review was not the equivalent of a modern appeal.

At its inception, King's Bench was a criminal court and a court of review over civil cases from Common Pleas. Most criminal acts, particularly those of a violent type, also involve civil aspects. If one, for instance, commits assault and battery, he is likely to be prosecuted criminally and to pay a fine or go to jail if found guilty. He is also subject to a civil suit for money damages by his victim. King's Bench had jurisdiction over the criminal aspect of such cases and, at the instance of the injured party, came by the reign of Edward I (1272-1307) to extend its jurisdiction to the civil side of the case. It took jurisdiction over the defendant because he had committed a breach of the king's peace, then dropped the criminal aspect and tried the civil suit.

Exchequer of Pleas. The Court of Exchequer of Pleas was the third of the common-law courts. The Exchequer was the treasury of the king. As part of its function it had, necessarily, to decide legal questions of tax liability to the Crown.

In addition it developed, around 1326, the famous procedure of the writ *quo minus,* which may have arisen in this way: A person was hailed before the Exchequer to answer a claim for taxes. He alleged that he would be glad to pay, but that he could not pay because John Doe owed him money and refused to pay him. Then the Exchequer would call John Doe before it to find out whether he actually owed the Crown's debtor the money. If he did, the Exchequer would order John Doe to pay.

It did not take ingenious minds long to discover that this was an ideal way to collect a debt. By using the Court of Exchequer of Pleas, the plaintiff had the full power of the Crown behind him. The obligation of John Doe, if found to be due, was owed to the court itself; therefore, the plaintiff did not have to follow the usual modes of execution on a judgment, but could have the Crown collect the money for him. The allegation that the plaintiff owed the Crown money became entirely fictitious and nontraversable (could not be denied). From this humble beginning, Exchequer of Pleas expanded its jurisdiction into complete civil coverage, a process which was completed by 1579. It also had certain equity functions which were not merged with those of the Court of Chancery until 1842.

The Court of Chancery—equity. The courts of Common Pleas, King's Bench, and Exchequer of Pleas developed the bulk of civil and criminal law. In part, this occurred by the invention of new writs, but much change came about through the stretching of existing concepts.

By the fifteenth century the system of law created by these courts was highly developed. Various circumstances combined, however, to slow down the process of further legal development and growth. Disturbed political conditions and internecine warfare made invention of new remedies inappropriate. The weight of the law itself gave rise to a disinclination to change. The common-law courts were created for a landed aristocracy, and the development of trade and commerce created needs for new remedies and ideas which were difficult to fit into the older remedies and theories based on land law.

In any event, appeals for extraordinary remedies were directed to the king and Council. This body, in accordance with usual administrative practice, referred certain matters to one of its members for action, and that member was the chancellor, the most important member of the Council. His office issued the writs which put the machinery of justice in motion in the common-law courts. The chancellor, before 1474, heard appeals for extraordinary remedies and related his recommendations back to the Council for final action. Sometimes he was instructed how to dispose of a case, but more often he made suggestions to the Council.

As a delegate of the Council, the chancellor enjoyed unusual powers. He could, for instance, issue the writ of subpoena which ordered parties to appear before him under penalty of imprisonment for refusal. In addition, he was not bound by the technical rules of pleading and procedure of the common-law courts. The Court of Chancery never had a jury. The chancellor could delegate his duty to hear cases to masters appointed by him, subject always to his review. Owing to its relative informality, to its background as a court of extraordinary relief, and to the clerical background of pre-Reformation chancellors, Chancery justice was likely to be more natural than the technical justice afforded by the common-law courts. The separate principles it developed became known as equitable rather than legal.

By 1474 Chancery had become a separate court. Its wide jurisdiction continued. Since its primary mission was to grant relief unobtainable in common-law courts because of a deficiency there of either theory or remedy, conflict with those courts was inevitable. In the first place, Chancery created new fields of law in areas left open by the common law, such as the enforcement of trusts, the law of fraud, and relief against penal clauses in contracts. Second, it created new remedies such as specific performance and injunctions. And third, it took upon itself more direct interference with common-law processes. On request of a petitioner who was being sued in a common-law court, for example, Chancery might order a litigant not to proceed in the common-law court. On occasion it would take a case already decided in the common-law courts and decide it anew, with the decision often going the other way. In such cases it would issue a writ of prohibition against the party who had won in the common-law court, forbidding him to proceed on the basis of that court's decision. These claims to supremacy were vindicated in the early seventeenth century by a royal commission. Although political considerations probably entered the commission's deliberations, the position taken doubtless was historically valid as far as Chancery's right to give extraordinary relief was concerned.

Since the chancellor was a Crown official, his office supported the claims of James I (1603-1625) and Charles I (1625-1649) to prerogative powers, that is, the claim that all governmental power stemmed from the king and, therefore, that Parliament and the common-law courts were subsidiary to him. Parliament, of course, opposed these claims. This struggle reached its climax and resulted in the execution of Charles I in 1649 and the abolition of the monarchy. For a time Parliament theoretically reigned supreme in a so-called Commonwealth period followed, in 1654, by a Protectorate headed by Oliver Cromwell, who held the title of Lord Protector and in fact, although not in theory, held dictatorial powers. Cromwell died in 1658, and virtual anarchy ensued until the restoration of the monarchy with the recall of the son of the executed king, who was crowned as Charles II in 1660. During the Commonwealth period,

Chancery went into eclipse, to regain its power only with the Restoration.

During the eighteenth and early nineteenth centuries, Chancery's rigidity in procedure and technicality in substance rivaled and even surpassed that of the common-law courts. In addition, the fact that it had only one chief officer, the chancellor, who might be asked to review any case decided by the masters in Chancery, made it intolerably slow. Final reform of Chancery procedure did not occur until the middle of the nineteenth century.

Proceedings in Chancery were begun by a bill, which differed from a writ in two significant ways. First, it had no set form and could be simply a general request for relief. Second, it issued directly from the court and did not require the approval of any other body. The bill device was also used in some of the cases before King's Bench.

Star Chamber.   The last of the major courts created before the parliamentary revolution of the seventeenth century was the Star Chamber. Its origin is uncertain, but it appears to have been the remnant of the medieval King's Council after the separation of Chancery from that body. The House of Lords had grown out of the Magna Curia long before 1474, and the House of Commons had been in existence for at least a century and a half by that time. Under Henry VII (1485-1509), the first of the Tudors, two acts were passed which either conferred or recognized Star Chamber's jurisdiction. The title Star Chamber came, apparently, from the name of the room in which the court sat. After the creation of the Privy Council to assist in executive matters in the 1530's, Star Chamber became purely a court. It dealt with matters involving magnates who might defy the regular courts, and with matters which threatened the security of the realm, such as criminal libel, conspiracy, forgery, and, later, fraud and the punishment of judges.

In its inception, Star Chamber was, in a true sense, a court of equity. That is, it granted, on principles of natural justice, remedies unavailable elsewhere. But its seventeenth century association with the king's prerogative, its application to criminal and political cases of equity's traditional broad and unchecked discretion, its use of torture to obtain evidence, and its often inhumane penalties made its later reputation somewhat less than enviable. It finally was abolished by Parliament in 1641 in the course of the disputes between Parliament and Charles I preliminary to the military revolution. With its passing, the original jurisdiction of the King's Council over legal matters disappeared. Star Chamber's jurisdiction passed into the hands of the other courts.

Church courts.   Until the Reformation, the church courts exercised jurisdiction over offenses against religion and morals, matrimonial matters, and the chattels of deceased persons. By the time of the Reformation their criminal jurisdiction had disappeared, and after that period their jurisdiction over decedents' personal property passed to the Court of Chancery.

The High Court of Parliament.   Basically the House of Lords sitting to try cases, the High Court of Parliament entertained proceedings in error from the King's Bench. The High Court's authority was based on the theory that the jurisdiction over errors of the King's Council was inherited by the House of Lords when it became distinct from the Council. Appeals from the Exchequer of Pleas went first, theoretically, to an Exchequer Chamber created in 1357, and appeals from this body were heard by the High Court of Parliament. It was not clear until the seventeenth century, however, that this court could hear appeals from Chancery.

Magna Carta stated that one was entitled to the judgment of his peers, and it referred, in part, to the right of peers of the realm to be tried by the King's Council. When the High Court of Parliament fell heir to the remnant of the Council's judicial authority, jurisdiction over the felonies and treasons of peers of the realm was a part of the inheritance, until the right was abolished by statute in 1948.

Conclusion. Our sketch of court development describes, essentially, a separation of the duties of government. The ancient King's Council was concerned with the totality of governmental affairs. Separation of the House of Lords and the addition of the House of Commons deleted its legislative function. Delegation of judicial duties to the courts of Common Pleas, King's Bench, and Exchequer of Pleas took away substantial judicial function, and much of the remainder was lodged in the chancellor when he became head of a separate court. Vestiges of judicial power remained in Star Chamber; but with its abolition, the judicial power of the medieval Council disappeared. The later Privy Council, product of a new theory of government, had no judicial power in England. It did, however, have judicial power to review decisions made by colonial courts, and therein lay the basis for conflict between the colonies and the mother country.

Modern English courts

The Judicature Act of 1873 initiated a series of statutes, culminating in the Supreme Court of Judicature (Consolidation) Act of 1925, which overturned the whole classical structure of the English courts. Modern England has two separate judicial branches, one for civil and one for criminal cases, often presided over by the same judges. No longer can the common-law courts and Chancery shoot legal arrows at each other, for they are part of the High Court of Justice, which is composed of the Queen's Bench Division, the Chancery Division, and the Probate, Divorce, and Admiralty Division.

American colonial courts

It was against the background of the English system that the American colonies and states created their own court structures. Neither their system of courts nor their law was adopted totally from the mother country, but they had no other experience to draw on. They were lower- and middle-class people whose day in court might have been on the manor or in the borough, and they knew little of the niceties of pleading and practice in the royal courts. Colonial law was not permitted to controvert the laws of England, but its proceedings attested to the fact that there was more law in England than that administered by the royal courts.

The colonies did not have a common system of court organization. Some colonies were royal, others were proprietary, and others were modeled after the joint stock trading companies. The colonies were differently settled—some by a fairly homogeneous community of religious dissidents, others by those who sought new opportunities to garner wealth, and yet other groups contained a fair proportion of the criminal element sent over to rid England of their presence.

Although generalities are impossible for the thirteeen colonies over the period of 175 years they were subject to England, a few observations can be made. English practice was followed in many ways. For instance, the colonies retained the local judiciary known as justices of the peace, or magistrates. In many colonies, justices of the peace sat a few times each year as minor criminal courts known as Courts of Quarter Sessions. As in England, they were not required to be learned in the law.

Terminology followed English usage in some places. Pennsylvania used and uses the term "Court of Common Pleas" for its civil trial courts, and Pennsylvania's and Virginia's major criminal courts were called Courts of Oyer and Terminer.

The ancient function of the king and his Council as the highest court was reproduced in many colonies by giving that function to the governor and his Council. A peculiarity of the colonial system, in addition, was that the king and Council in England heard appeals from judgments of the highest courts of many colonies.

On the other hand, colonial conditions caused many changes from English practice. Separate courts of equity or Chancery were late developments, and early colonial courts administered equity and law side by side in the same courts. Simplicity was also demonstrated by the colonial treatment of procedure and evidence, in which—from a combination of lack of training and distaste for the refined technicalities of English practice—elasticity replaced rigidity and substance tended to conquer form.

By the nineteenth century, however, the growth of a better-trained bar brought with it a return to more complicated forms of law and procedure. The importation of English law books, from Littleton to Blackstone, accelerated this process. But some judicial opinions observe that despite the respect in which earlier judges are held, their inadequate learning makes their judgments entitled to little weight. Some of the legislatures in the newer western colonies so deeply deplored the trend to follow English law that they forbade the citation of English cases in their courts. The urge to examine English law for relevant precedents was, however, impossible to resist during the formative period of our own law. There was no other example, realistically, to follow, and the dominant feeling of the times was that law was something more than the opinion of the judges—that there was some general common law which all courts should follow and which, therefore, might well be found in English cases.

By the middle of the nineteenth century, the preconditions of a separate and distinct jurisprudence had been met: sufficient American precedents had developed, texts had been written, and lawyers had been trained. Although English law continued to be searched for precedents where American law was lacking, those areas became fewer and fewer as the years went by.

1963
1923
40

The jury

3

CURSED, REVILED, BLESSED, OR PRAISED, the jury has stood firm for seven hundred years. So firmly did our forefathers uphold the jury that we find the right to jury trial anchored in our federal and state constitutions.

There are two types of juries. The first, the petit jury, is used in both civil and criminal cases. In civil cases its task is generally to determine liability to pay money damages; in criminal cases its task is to determine punishable guilt, and it usually does so with a minimum of criticism. There its position as a bulwark of liberty, a protector against executive oppression, and a mode of lessening the rigors of too-strict legislation is secure. In England, where the use of the civil jury has been greatly reduced by legislation, the criminal jury remains in its traditional form.

The civil jury, however, is subject to much criticism. It appears, sometimes, to be a means whereby individuals can obtain unjust judgments against corporate defendants, for the jury may tend to ally itself with the underdog. The jury is, in many instances, incompetent to handle involved testimony, particularly on technical matters. In this country, nevertheless, accusations of bias, incompetence, capriciousness, unpredictability, delay, and expense usually have gone unheeded.

The trial jury, to speak for the moment in its defense, is presented with a difficult task. It must reconstruct history. It must determine the facts of a past transaction. If its verdicts seem excessive, one must keep in mind the impossibility of determining the money value of such intangibles as pain and suffering or loss of reputation. Any criticism of the jury must also take into account possible alternative methods of finding facts. And in such deliberations it must not be forgotten that jury verdicts do not create precedents.

The second type of jury is the grand jury. It differs from the trial or petit jury in that it does not decide questions of guilt or innocence. Its function is accusatory. When a possible offender is brought before a magistrate, and the magistrate believes there is suspicion of guilt, the matter is presented to the grand jury for investigation. If the grand jury finds enough evidence to warrant a trial, it will issue a true bill of indictment and the case will proceed. If the evidence is insufficient, the case will be dismissed. On occasion, the grand jury is charged with a special commission to investigate specific types of possible criminal activity among the general population or among governmental officials, and such investigations may also result in indictments. The grand jury has been abolished in England and in approximately one-half of our states. Its existence, however, is guaranteed by the Constitution in federal cases.

Both types of juries fit the classic definition given by Sir Frederick Maitland many years ago: that a jury is a body of neighbors summoned under oath to answer questions of fact.[1] The trial jury answers the question of guilt or innocence, liability or nonliability; the grand jury determines whether there is enough evidence to warrant a criminal trial. Not only do these juries fit the same definition, but they derive, ultimately and in the distant past, from the same origins.

Origins of the jury

The foundation of the jury system goes back a thousand years to the French empire of the Carolingian kings. Those monarchs, as part of their successful attempt to unite their empire, developed a procedure called the inquest, or inquisition, to determine the nature and extent of royal rights. They called together the people of the countryside and required them to relate their understanding of the immemorial rights of the king. The rights being ascertained, they were adopted by the central administration. There was neither accusation, verdict, nor judgment in these proceedings, but the inquest fixed the right of the state to obtain information from its citizens.

Norman use of the inquest. The Norman invaders were not long on English soil before they used the inquest, again for royal purposes, in the compilation of Domesday Book, a census of the ownership of all the land in England. It listed landowners, of whom the land was held in accordance with feudal theory, the chattels on the land, and other information. Its purpose was to establish the base for the imposition of taxes and feudal dues. Its name perhaps arose out of popular opinion that the inquiry was as thorough as that to be visited upon men on the Day of Judgment.

---

[1] Frederick Pollock and F. W. Maitland, *The History of English Law before the Time of Edward I*, 2nd ed. (Cambridge: Cambridge University Press, 1952), II, 138.

For another use of the inquest we must turn to the criminal jurisdiction of the communal courts. Since a person cannot be tried for a crime, unless he is first accused, four men from each vill and twelve from each hundred appeared before the County Court and voluntarily accused individuals of specific crimes. They were not summoned by a public officer, however, so they did not meet Maitland's definition of a jury.

This voluntary procedure was made compulsory by the Assize of Clarendon, a "statute" of 1166. It came to be called a presenting jury and was the predecessor of our modern grand jury.

The possessory assizes. In 1166, Henry II instituted the possessory assizes, a new type of procedure for the settling of disputes concerning land. Under the prior writ of right, a person had to prove the older title to land; and if the facts were in doubt, trial by combat—a physical encounter between champions hired by the plaintiff and by the defendant—decided the matter. This action gave a great advantage to the defendant. Having taken the land of the plaintiff, perhaps by violent means, he could sit back and wait for the plaintiff to prove older title to it and, when the issue was finally joined, overwhelm the plaintiff by the force, not of argument, but of expensive hired champions.

A remedy for this intolerable situation was provided by the possessory assizes, whereby the plaintiff had only to show that he was the last possessor of the land and that he had been disseised, or dispossessed, by the defendant. At that point the defendant was required to restore the plaintiff to possession. There was no question of the older ownership which, if still contested, could be settled by the writ of right. This, however, rarely occurred. Nor was there battle. The writ directed the empaneling of an inquest or assize, a group of neighbors who were presumably well enough acquainted with the facts to decide whether the disseisin had taken place. Instead of submitting the crucial question of disseisin to the hazardous fortunes of an armed conflict, it was submitted to the body most likely to know what had happened—the neighbors of the litigants. This inquest differed from our jury in that it could not be waived.

Around 1179 the assize procedure was also made optional with the defendant under the older writ of right. The plaintiff, however, still had to prove the older title to the land and not mere dispossession.

It is tempting to consider this jury of twelve used in the various possessory assizes and in the writ of right as the progenitor of the modern petit jury, but this would be inaccurate. The possessory assizes met a distinct need and were used for some centuries, but our modern jury has its direct origin elsewhere. The jury of the possessory assizes died without successors.

The petit jury and the ordeals. For the source of the modern trial or petit jury we must turn again to the presenting jury instituted by the Assize of Clarendon in 1166.[2] Having been presented, how were the ac-

---

[2] The word "assize" was variously applied in early English law. Basically, it meant a meeting of people. Thus a jury could be called an assize. Or it could mean action

cused persons to be tried? In accordance with ancient pagan practice, to which the forms of Christianity had been added, many people were tried by ordeals. Some were absolved on their oaths, supported by the aid of "oathhelpers" required by the court, who would swear that the defendant was a truthful man. This was called wager of law.

The ordeal was an appeal to the supernatural to determine the guilt or innocence of the accused. There were various ordeals, all based on the idea that God would disclose the guilt or innocence of the accused. There was the ordeal of cold water, in which the accused was secured by a rope and let down into a pool. If the water received him and he sank, he was thereby proved innocent. There was the ordeal of the hot iron, in which the accused carried a red-hot iron for a certain distance, at the end of which his hand was bound. If in three days it contained no unclean matter, he was thereby proved innocent. In the ordeal of the cursed morsel, the accused swallowed a piece of dry bread with a feather in it; if he did not choke on the bread, he was proved innocent. All these ordeals were administered amidst the ritual of the Church at the high moment of the Mass. Oddly enough, evidence from early cases indicates a preponderance of acquittals when the ordeals were used, perhaps because of the invitation of this mode of litigation to corrupt practices.

Speculation concerning the psychological aspects of the ordeal as an instrument to determine truth is doubtless futile, and it may be sufficient to say that the high powers of the Church were not at all satisfied with the Church's participation. In 1215 the Fourth Lateran Council forbade priests to take part in trials by ordeal. The criminal law of England was consequently made unworkable—the chief method of finding facts in criminal cases was gone. In remote places priests disobeyed the order and continued to participate in ordeals, but in general the prohibition was obeyed.

What alternative remained for the finding of the facts? Let the judge do it? Impossible! He would be replacing the voice of God in the ordeals. After toying with a temporary expedient which imprisoned those of evil repute, banished those guilty of intermediate crimes, and required pledges of security from those accused of lesser offenses, judges began to resort to the presenting juries. At the gatherings of the court were presenting juries from every vill and hundred. Some of them were acquainted with the alleged offense—indeed their members may have been the accusers. What would be more natural than to ask their opinions? A number of jurors, perhaps as many as forty-eight, would be asked whether the accused was guilty or innocent. They decided, not on the basis of testimony or evidence presented to them, but on the basis of their own knowledge or what they could find out.

Since this procedure was an innovation, the accused could not be required to submit to it. Instead, he was asked whether he would "put

---

taken by a meeting; therefore, if the council met at a given place, the action taken there could be called an assize, as the Assize of Clarendon. The sessions of court held by royal justices, being meetings, were also called assizes.

himself upon the country," as the saying went. If he refused, his guilt might never be decided, for the procedure could not then be used.

In an attempt to end the impasse, the Statute of Westminster I (1275) provided that if the accused refused to submit to a jury, he should be put in a strong and fast prison (*prison forte et dure*). A peculiar change in meaning occurred, whereby this phrase came to mean *peine forte et dure*, a legal torture in which the accused was loaded with heavy weights of iron until he either submitted to trial by jury or expired. If he died without trial under this torture, he had not been found guilty, and therefore his chattels were not forfeited to the Crown. In this way, he could heroically save his family from the financial consequences of his punishment. This rule was not changed in England until 1772.

Prisoners were reluctant to submit to the jury because it was composed, in part at least, of the very persons who had accused him. A verdict of guilty, it seems, was assured beforehand. This difficulty was removed, however, in 1351 or 1352, when it was determined that the trial jury should not include any members of the presenting jury that had accused the defendant, if the defendant chose to challenge their presence. The jury, however, still spoke of its own knowledge and did not hear witnesses until about one hundred years later.

Attaint of jurors.   Because jurors spoke of their own knowledge until about 1450, it was possible that a jury might knowingly come to a false verdict. A judge who suspected that one had done so could appoint an attainting jury of twenty-four persons to try the members of the first jury for their perjury. If found guilty, they could be imprisoned, and their chattels could be forfeited to the Crown. When jurors ceased to speak of their own knowledge, this procedure became obsolete.

In the sixteenth century, in an attempt to solve the problem of favoritism toward defendants, particularly those accused of political crimes, juries were made amenable to the process of other courts, including the Star Chamber. In addition, they might be fined heavily for contempt if they refused to follow the instructions of a judge in a criminal case.

Chief Justice Vaughan, in *Bushel's Case* (1670), determined that a jury was not in contempt for refusing to follow such instructions. His reasoning was ingenious. He said that since jurors were already subject to the penalty of attaint for a false verdict, they must be free to come to their own independent conclusions; otherwise they would not be responsible for their verdict. What he said was true in theory because attaint of juries had never been formally abolished, but it was no longer true in fact. By appealing to this nonexistent theory, he succeeded in freeing the jury from political compulsion.

Role of Magna Carta.   Contrary to popular conception, Magna Carta had little or nothing to do with the inception of the jury. The "judgment of his peers" (*judicium parium suorum*) of Magna Carta refers to the ancient system of trying nobles in a court consisting of their fellow nobles, a custom which continued into modern times in the English House of Lords. It also referred, in civil cases, to the jury used in the possessory assizes, which, by the sixteenth century, had fallen into disuse.

To the extent, however, that Magna Carta opposed the unbridled power of the Crown and expressed the rule of law rather than of men, it had an indirect but very real effect on the retention of the jury system. The tinted view of subsequent generations that Magna Carta was the source of the jury was, although incorrect, extremely important in enabling it to withstand criticism in times of stress.

Extension of the jury system. From these sources the modern criminal jury ultimately developed. And out of it, in turn, developed the civil jury. This curious circumstance came about because King's Bench, during the course of the fourteenth and fifteenth centuries, developed a civil jurisdiction based on an extension of its jurisdiction over trespass to cover civil damages, explained in Chapter 2. By other devices King's Bench also adopted some of the writs used by the Court of Common Pleas. As it extended its business into the civil area, it used the jury for fact-finding purposes in civil cases.

In the meantime, though with less success, Common Pleas used equivalent fictions and subterfuges in civil cases to employ remedies that had been developed in King's Bench. In so doing, it adopted the jury used by King's Bench in these actions. Only the older actions relied on wager of law, the ancient method of fact-finding.

Equity, however, including the Court of Chancery, never adopted the jury system. Suits in equity were not derived from the actions developed in the common-law courts.

Present status of the jury

Today the grand jury exists in only half the United States and in the federal courts. Since 1933 it has existed in England for only a few types of cases, and it does not exist in civil-law countries. The petit jury exists in all our states and in the federal courts, although it often is waived in technical cases on concurrence of both parties. It exists in England in criminal cases, but in only a few types of civil cases. In civil-law countries it is not used in civil cases at all, although in some civil-law countries a petit jury is occasionally used in criminal cases.

The modern alternative to the grand jury is accusation by information.[3] The district attorney or other appropriate official directly orders the criminal court to try a criminal case. Under the information procedure, prosecution of a criminal case depends on the decision of the district attorney's office.

Conclusion

From this résumé of the evolution of the jury system it should be apparent that there is nothing in its history to require

---

[3] Informations were used in early England, particularly by the Council and Star Chamber.

its indefinite continuance. From an instrument of royal oppression it became a means of protection against state interference. But this change was the happenstance of situation and not the product of intrinsic merit or planned growth. For cases in which the jury meets modern needs, it should be continued. For cases in which it does not, it should be eliminated. Whatever substitute may be found for the jury, however, the basic problem of reconstructing the history of a transaction will remain. A more professional technique of fact determination, therefore, may not necessarily result in greater speed, impartiality, wisdom, or truth.

The bench and bar

LAWYERS ARE A HARDY GROUP. IN THE FACE of criticism, cynicism, and pleas for their abolition, they have survived. When a lawyer submits to occupational temptations, the public is indignant; but criticism is sometimes the voice of ignorance, the layman's misunderstanding of technicalities.

Functions of lawyers

Lawyers survive because people need their two important functions: advice and advocacy. Advising, or counseling, is an informal, often personal, function. The lawyer drafts a will, assists in the buying of a house, starting a small business, or forming a large corporation. Advocacy is a formal function by which the lawyer represents and speaks for his client—usually before a court or administrative body—but advocacy may include representation in other forms also.

Some lawyers specialize in courtroom work, others may never appear on that scene, but all lawyers in the United States are authorized to perform both functions: counseling and advocacy. In England, the bar always has been separated into barristers, who appear in court, and solicitors (formerly called attorneys), who mainly engage in office practice, although they may appear in lesser courts. France maintains the English distinction, and the *avocat* is the French equivalent of the barrister; the *avouet* is the solicitor.

Modern legal education

French lawyers are trained in universities, and American legal education is almost uniformly postgraduate professional education at a formal law school, usually affiliated with a university. English barristers, on the other hand, enter the profession as members of one of four Inns of Court, which are combinations of a law school and a professional organization. It is at the Inns that they obtain their legal education. Solicitors are trained under the auspices of the Law Society, which sees to their practical training and to the completion of one year of formal legal training.

Judges in the United States, with exceptions in the minor judiciary, are selected from the ranks of lawyers. In England they are chosen from the select group of barristers known as Queen's Counsel. In France, however, the beginning law student must make a choice between the bench and the bar. If he chooses the judiciary, his education is distinct from that of prospective members of the bar. He must first complete a law school program and then take an examination for admission to the National Center of Judicial Studies, where he undergoes one year of practical training and two years of study. The neophyte judge may start his career as a magistrate in a province and slowly work up within the civil service to the larger cities and more impressive posts. The French lawyer, trained in a law school, plunges immediately into practice, and his ultimate goals cannot include the judiciary.

The diverse training and careers of common- and civil-law judges is significant. Similar backgrounds and experience provide a certain feeling of fellowship and mutual sympathy between the common-law bench and bar. The presiding judge can view the arguments of counsel with understanding, for he may have used them himself on a prior day. The contending counsel can appreciate the qualities of the judge, for they may have practiced with him or against him in the past. The prestige of the English and American judiciary is much greater than that of their civil-law counterparts, partly because of the general feeling that only the best lawyers get judicial posts. The politics of appointment and election notwithstanding, this conclusion probably is generally true.

Origins of the bar

The origins of the bar are found in necessity. Until the body of legal knowledge, including procedure, had become too much for the ordinary person to handle for himself, there was no need for a legal profession. But by the time of Henry II (1154-1189) it was possible for a litigant to appoint someone to do his technical pleading. This person, the *responsalis*, was not a member of a separate profession, for apparently anyone could act in that capacity. He eventually developed into, or was superseded by, the attorney who was appointed in court and had the power to bind his employer to a plea. By the thirteenth century, attorneys constituted a recognized profession.

Just as technical pleading required the aid of an attorney, so oral argument came to require special skill. The privilege of appearing in person before the king's justices became a hollow and dangerous one as the law became more technical. By the time of Henry III (1216-1272) judges had become professionals, and the courts had started to create a body of substantive legal knowledge as well as technical procedure. The narrators, or pleaders, came into being to speak for litigants in court and to perform the function of advocacy.

The king had need of persons to represent his interests in the courts. In the early fourteenth century, he appointed sergeants of the king (*servientes regis*) to take care of his legal business. When not engaged in the king's business, these fabled sergeants-at-law of the Common Pleas court could serve individuals, and they superseded the narrators.

But perhaps the crucial event in the beginning of the legal profession was an edict issued in 1292 by Edward I. At that time what passed for a profession was in a sorry state. Legal business had increased tremendously; yet there were no schools of the common law, and the universities considered law too vulgar a subject for scholarly investigation. Edward's order, which directed Common Pleas to choose certain "attorneys and learners" who alone would be allowed to follow the court and to take part in court business, created a monopoly of the legal profession.

The effect of putting the education of lawyers into the hands of the court cannot be overestimated. It resulted in the relative isolation of English lawyers from Continental, Roman, and ecclesiastical influence. Lawyer taught lawyer, and each learned from the processes of the courts, so that the law had to grow by drawing on its own resources and not by borrowing from others. It became insular. Whether this was good or bad for the development of the law is a debatable question, but it did create a unique system with a minimum of foreign ideas.

Obviously the court itself was no place for the training of these attorneys and learners. The court did offer aid in providing an observation post, called the crib, in which students could sit and take notes and from which, occasionally, they might ask questions during the course of the trial.

The Inns of Court. The custom of lawyers living together during terms of court, dating back as far as Magna Carta (1215), gave rise to the unique English institution of the Inns of Court. The first, the Honorable Society of Lincoln's Inn, was given a home in the reign of Edward I (1272-1307). Its preserved records date from 1422. Sometime later, Inner Temple, Middle Temple, and Gray's Inn were established. At more than a dozen of these Inns, lawyers and students lived and were taught the tradition and learning of the common law. The Inns were subject to supervision by the judges and were associated with the Inns of Chancery.

Since the Inns also taught things such as music and dancing, it was not uncommon to find members who did not intend to enter the legal profession. Those who did, however, had a long and arduous training. The entering student, after two years of instruction in elementary law as a member of an Inn of Chancery, was admitted to the Inn of Court to which it was attached. For the next four or five years he was trained first in answering legal questions and second in arguing moot cases. At that point, he became an inner barrister and could look forward to another eight years of training. Only then was he called to the bar as an utter (or outer) barrister and permitted to practice before King's Bench. He might also at this point be chosen as a reader to give lectures to members of the Inn. But only after more experience might he be chosen a sergeant-at-law and permitted to practice before the oldest of the courts, Common Pleas, as well as before King's Bench. Sergeants were not permitted to teach, but received the highest fees. Their order was abolished in 1877.

For a time, inner barristers could act as attorneys, and until the 1500's, when they were expelled, many attorneys were attached to the Inns of Court. If attorneys acted for fees, they were required (by a series of statutes beginning with the order of Edward I in 1292) to be approved by the judges. In the eighteenth century, the name "attorney" was dropped in favor of the term "solicitor," with the formation of the Society of Gentlemen Practicers in the Courts of Law and Equity, which was their professional society until 1903, when the Law Society came into being.

American lawyers

In the New World there appears never to have been a time when the profession was divided into solicitors and barristers. The English division was part of a social system which did not exist, at least in its full rigor, in the New World. The small size of the colonies likewise made such a system unnecessary.

The practitioner of Colonial times, and often as late as the 1920's, commonly was a person who had studied his craft in the office of another lawyer, known as his preceptor. He was not necessarily a college graduate. Some Colonial lawyers had attended the English Inns of Court, and many later lawyers were college graduates, but these accomplishments were not essential. Court approval for admission was, however, a requirement.

Law schools in this country, except for the famous school at Litchfield, Connecticut, which existed from 1784 to 1833, received their real impetus after the Civil War. Some advances made in the 1830's created the base for subsequent development. Today a degree from an approved law school is a common requirement for admission to the bar, although the apprenticeship route is still open, theoretically, in a number of states. A few states require a short period of apprenticeship in addition to a law degree.

The bench

The mystery of the common-law judges can easily be presented but is much more difficult to explain. It is this: the judges of England started as the king's men, representing his personal interests, and ended as protectors of the citizenry against the king's prerogative.

This metamorphosis was not complete until the seventeenth century, and it was a change which profoundly affected Anglo-American law.

There were no true judges outside the royal courts. In the communal and seignorial courts there were only suitors who performed the judicial function but were not professionals because they were neither career men nor specially trained. Even the early justices of the king were not professional judges, because they acted on an *ad hoc* basis.

Earliest judges. The first true judges emerged with the Common Pleas court at the end of the twelfth century. Their positions were far from secure: since they were selected from the men immediately serving the king, they were subject to his whim for both appointment and removal. Until the middle of the thirteenth century most of them were in clerical orders, although not necessarily involved with clerical duties. Their ability to hold church office and to receive the proceeds thereof enabled even those in the lowest orders to enter the service of the king, who paid low and often uncertain compensation. Clerical status assumed a certain minimum of education, including the ability to read and write— accomplishments not often shared even by the nobility.

In the church courts, *ad hoc* delegates, who spent most of their time in their own pursuits, were appointed for particular cases. Had the common law adopted such a system, the development of a full-time professional judiciary would have been considerably delayed.

The common-law system of choosing judges from the king's favorites worked with a fair degree of efficiency until the reign of Henry III (1216-1272). That reign, however, was marked by another revolt of the barons, more devastating than the rebellion which led to Magna Carta in the immediately prior reign of King John. Simon de Montfort, Earl of Leicester, was successful in reducing Henry III to political impotence after the Battle of Lewes in 1264, and the victory was followed by the creation of a Council of Magnates to rule the realm. This unrest, which began around 1256, ended only with the accession of Edward I (1272-1307).

The unrest had an unfortunate effect on the judiciary. Bracton stopped writing his remarkable law book around 1256, complaining that the judges had so deteriorated in quality that to find good English law he was forced to look back to Pateshull and Raleigh, the judicial masters of the 1220's. And in 1289 Edward I found it necessary to purge the judiciary. Scandalous reports were made concerning the judges, involving allegations of corruption, bribery, murder, and other heinous crimes. A special commission was appointed by the King to look into the matter, and many of the charges were sustained. As one result, the Chief Justice of Common Pleas fled the country.

During this time important legal advances had nonetheless taken place. Reform began with the Statute of Marlborough in 1267 and continued through the Statute of Westminster I (1275), the Statute of Gloucester (1284), and the vast Statute of Westminster II (1285). In total, these statutes constituted a revolution in substantive and procedural law.

During or immediately after this period a practice arose of the utmost importance to Anglo-American law: judges were chosen not from the king's favorites, but from eminent sergeants-at-law. Henceforth practicing lawyers were to be the sole source of the higher judiciary. This meant that a community of interest between the bench and the bar would exist to a closer degree than in any other legal system. When in 1292 legal education was entrusted to the judges, the system became totally inbred. Lawyers taught prospective lawyers, judges were selected from lawyers, and judges supervised legal education. This system proved to have a high degree of resistance to foreign ideas and to purely academic theorizing.

Independence of the judiciary. The judges selected from the lawyers were still, however, appointed only during the king's pleasure (*durante bene placito*). It was only with the Act of Settlement in 1701 that they came to be appointed for so long as they behaved themselves well (*quamdiu se bene gesserint*). Their salaries became certain at that time, and joint action of both houses of Parliament became necessary in order to remove judges from office.

Between 1455 and 1461 the fratricidal Wars of the Roses took place. The swiftly changing fortunes of battle made impolitic, if not impossible, judicial alignment with any particular faction. As a result, the judiciary remained immune from political interference, and a strong precedent was created for the removal of judges from politics. The risk of such interference, however, again became apparent in connection with Queen Mary's attempt to restore Roman Catholicism (1553-1558).

Lord Coke, during his struggles with James I (1603-1625), laid a further basis for the independence of the judiciary. Two cases decided by that memorable jurist, who at one time or another during his life held nearly every important English legal post, stand as firm precedents for the rule of law and the supremacy of the courts. In *Dr. Bonham's Case,* Lord Coke subjected Parliament to the law with the statement that "when an Act of Parliament is against Common right and reason, or repugnant, or impossible to be performed, the Common Law will control it and adjudge such Act to be void." [1] In the *Case of Proclamations,* Coke and his brethren on the bench gave their opinion to King James that the king was without power to make law. The result was Coke's elevation to the office of Chief Justice of King's Bench, where his views presumably would not be so detrimental to the interests of the King. He was, however, dismissed from that office in 1616, and ultimately he went into politics.

The revolution which ended the reign of James II (1685-1688) formally determined the question of judicial independence for all time. That bloodless conflict ended with the supremacy of Parliament established, and with it the independence of the courts. The Act of Settlement of 1701 recognized the existing fact.

---

[1] 8 Rep. 118a (1610). Despite this dictum, no English court has ever held an English statute to be unconstitutional.

➣ PART II

Sources
of
Law

Custom and cases

5

FOR A TECHNICAL BODY OF LAW TO EXIST, there must be some distinct group of persons, a legal profession, to develop it. Such a profession emerges slowly; and in the beginning of any legal system, law is nothing more or less than the customary rules of the community.

Custom and law

Twelfth-century England was ruled by custom. Each manor, each county, and perhaps even each vill had its own customs. The powers of the royal government were customary also. And custom at that time did not have to be immemorially old to be enforced as law. A custom, it was said, was old if it had existed for ten years, very old if for twenty, and ancient if it was thirty years old. Communities could and did adopt customs wholesale from other communities.

Changes in customs controlling the constitution of government, including the courts, created the legal profession. The separation of the judiciary from the council, the nature of the writ system, the procedure of the courts, the emergence of barristers and attorneys —all were accomplished as changes in custom. Legislation, in the modern sense, was still in the future.

When the legal profession came into existence, it had either to choose its newly emerging law from the mass of customs in existence or else to create new customs. Slowly, custom became what was accepted by the royal courts, not the general population. Custom still ruled at local levels where royal law did not intervene and was enforced in the manors, for instance, until the beginnings of the modern period.

The common law was, therefore, the customs of the royal courts. It was this law which became the object of study by the legal profession. As time passed, lawyers began to view unfavorably the idea that outside custom could change the law. By the 1500's it had become the accepted rule that for a custom of the country to be accepted by the courts, it had to be immemorially old; and the date chosen was September 3, 1189, the coronation of Richard I.

One consequence of this rule was to slow the change from the ancient estates of villeinage to copyhold estates. The old estates of villeins were protected only in the manor courts, not in the royal courts. The Black Death (1348-1349) which so reduced the population of England naturally brought about changes in the social order. One result was that erstwhile villeins had been able to extract more favorable conditions of landholding, called copyhold estates, from the lords. But the royal courts, by requiring proof that there was a custom of copyhold estates on the manor involved dating back to 1189, arrested this shift for a time. As a matter of fact, there were no copyholds in England in 1189.

Pockets of custom persisted in some parts of England and were enforced in the royal courts. One of the most famous of these is the custom known as borough English, under which land devolved upon the youngest rather than the eldest son. This particular usage was abolished only in the twentieth century.

Custom today has slight effect in case law. Meanings of technical terms in contracts, for instance, are defined by custom, and knowledge of commercial custom can often assist a judge in mercantile cases.[1] It does have a compelling effect on legislation in areas in which prior law has been outrun by events. Commercial custom has forced many changes in statutes, and this will be considered subsequently in the treatment of commercial law.

Cases as a source of law

Modern American courts assure the careful reporting and publishing of their decisions and opinions by appointing official reporters to make verbatim transcriptions. This accurate law-case reporting, however, began only in the nineteenth century. Until the reign of Edward I (1272-1307), there was no single place to look for cases. The law books referred to them, tradition carried them forward, and the plea rolls of the courts contained some information, but the exact wording of the decisions was eternally lost.

The Year Books. In Edward I's reign, the compilation of Year Books

---

[1] The importance of custom in the reception of mercantile law by the courts is discussed in the section, "Early Mercantile Law," in Chapter 11.

began a three-century practice. In their first century, the volumes were extremely informal, doubtless collections by year of informal notes taken by lawyers and students of cases. Books were not usually organized according to subject matter, they had no official approval, but they were collected because they were useful to the profession. There was no attempt to include all cases, and comments dealt with judges' personalities and lawyers' quips as often as with matters of legal substance. The notes of cases, obtained from diverse persons, had no common form.

In the fifteenth century, the Year Books became more professional and uniform. They were still by no means official, nor did they report cases as soon as they were decided (some cases might be two or three years old), but they seem to have entered upon a period of more serious reporting.[2] Their compilation ceased in 1535.

When the Year Books had begun to amass numerous cases, Abridgments appeared. They were compilations, usually condensed, of cases reported in the Year Books but arranged by subject matter, apparently to facilitate study, and many of them were produced by students as so-called commonplace books for practice in abstracting cases and in analysis.

Some Abridgments were printed. The earliest of these is one attributed to Statham, at the very end of the fifteenth century. Later published Abridgments obtained more fame, from Fitzherbert's (1516), down to the twenty-three volumes of Viner's Abridgment, published between 1742 and 1753. It was Viner who endowed Blackstone's chair at Oxford.

Private reporters. Immediately after the cessation of the Year Books, individually printed reports appeared. Privately published for individual advantage or profit, they still were not official. Different reports covered the same periods and cases. Dyer's reports, for instance, ran from 1537 to 1582 and were duplicated in part by the reports of Plowden, who covered the years 1550 to 1580.

Reports varied in quality. Some of them were of such low reputation that particular judges forbade them to be cited in court; others were most reliable. Variations often appear in the same case reported by different reporters, giving the researcher considerable difficulty. Cases were usually published long after they were decided; current reports awaited the end of the eighteenth century.

Although England still does not have strictly official reports, the United States began to appoint official reporters at the beginning of the nineteenth century. Apparently, the American practice started with the United States Supreme Court in the early 1800's; the states followed at irregular intervals. All states fell in line by the Civil War. Official reports are the only ones which can be cited with authority in the courts, although copies of them are published by private publishing houses (cases being in the public domain and not the subject of copyright).

The doctrines of precedent and stare decisis. In any developed legal system, cases are a source of law. The question, however, is the relative

---

[2] Theodore F. T. Plucknett, *A Concise History of the Common Law,* 5th ed. (Boston: Little, Brown & Co., 1956), pp. 271-72.

importance given to them, in comparison with the weight given to statutes and treatises.

The Anglo-American legal system traditionally adheres to the doctrine of *stare decisis*. If a judge finds a prior case decided by the highest court of his jurisdiction in which the facts are not distinguishably different, he must follow it if the decision is still in the spirit of the times. The highest court of a given jurisdiction must either follow its own prior decision or overrule it. In England the doctrine is very strict, for there the highest court cannot overrule its own prior decision.

The French, rejecting this doctrine, deride it as *la superstition du cas*. French judges nevertheless are affected, although not in a binding manner, by a series of decisions which indicates the nature of their law. This is called *la jurisprudence*.

Sometimes the doctrine of *stare decisis* is referred to as the doctrine of precedent, but there is a difference, historically, between the use of precedents and adherence to the doctrine of *stare decisis*.

The idea of looking back to prior cases for guidance is as old as our professional courts. In 1256 Bracton did this but chose to reject some cases as "bad law," while accepting others. He did not find law from the cases, but illustrated law by the use of cases. During the Middle Ages, in the period of the Year Books, prior cases were also inspected, but scarcely revered. Law was not found in a single case; rather, a group of cases illustrated the true law. Law, in this sense, was the total custom of the courts.

There are at least three reasons why a doctrine of *stare decisis* could not have been developed before the nineteenth century. The first is that the general tenor of thinking was distinctly hostile to the idea that a judge could *make* law. Law was something higher than the pronouncements of any court. A decision was merely evidence of the law—the best evidence, perhaps, but nothing more than that. Only in the second quarter of the nineteenth century, with the positivist jurisprudence of John Austin, did thinking on this matter start to change. Austin's concept of law as a command of the sovereign substituted the theory that the judges *made* law for the prior theory that they merely *declared* the law. Austin's teaching is by no means the end of the tale on that subject, but it created the intellectual climate needed for the doctrine of *stare decisis*.

The second reason is that there was no truly reliable system of reporting cases before the nineteenth century. Assuming a case is law, one must know definitively what it says. The Year Books of the Middle Ages did not purport to be complete, and the individual reports varied in reliability. In England, semiofficial reports did not appear until 1865, although they appeared considerably earlier in the same century in this country.

And last, there was no distinct hierarchy of courts, with one highest court in each jurisdiction, until the late eighteenth century. There must be a single voice to declare the law. In the United States this event occurred earlier than it did in England. The federal Constitution of 1789 created the Supreme Court, and the various state constitutions did the same. In England there was no one highest court until 1873.

For these three reasons, there was no firm doctrine of *stare decisis* in the United States before 1800. By 1825 some of the older states had started to stress the binding power of a single prior decision, and by 1850 the doctrine was firmly entrenched.

Today the doctrine is in full force in England, but in the United States it is discernibly beginning to break down. The number of reported cases is too great for any lawyer or judge adequately to handle, and the tendency is, once more, to search for principles rather than single precedents. As usual, practice precedes theory, and the theory still is that one case from the highest court binds a similar later case in the same jurisdiction.

Legislation and codification

LEGISLATION IS THE MOST POTENT MEANS for changing law. Case law tends, by its nature, to lag behind the times. Legislation can and does bring about abrupt changes in many areas; but where matters political, social, or religious are involved, legislation is not highly successful.

Origins of legislation

Legislation has a long and honorable tradition. Roman legislation began in the assemblies of the republic, developed through statutes passed by the Senate at the instance of the emperor, and finally became blatantly imperial.

The Anglo-Saxons, from A.D. 600 onward, enacted much that may be viewed as legislation, although a significant portion of it was a recording of pre-existing custom. William the Conqueror and his Council enacted a good deal of legislation, but real impetus came with the reign of Henry II (1154-1189). Legislation was referred to by various names—assizes, constitutions, provisions, and charters. An assize was a meeting, but sometimes the statute that came out of it was also called an assize. Collections of old laws and customs were gathered into constitutions and provisions. A charter, as the name implies, was a grant of rights and privileges, but it may have been merely declaratory of old rights and privileges. Magna Carta, revised four times between 1215 and 1225, was such a document.

The addition of the House of Commons. The end of the thirteenth century brings us closer to modern legislation. Earlier legislation had taken the form of a grant of rights and privileges by the king and his Council, but under Edward I it became a concurrence of action by the king and the newly emerging Parliament. The word "parliament" means a gathering of persons for the purpose of discussion—holding a parley. Beginning in 1213, representatives of the communes or communities (the shires and boroughs) were called to meet with King John and his Council for the purpose of consenting to measures he desired—particularly when his finances were involved. Since war was the main cause of financial emergencies, it may be credited with spurring the growth of representative government. Another source was the ancient right of the king to grant redress of grievances, which came to be presented by the representatives of the commoners in their meetings with the king and his Council.

Edward I (1272-1307) introduced the procedure of petition and grant. Petitions from representatives of the commons were referred to the chancellor, the judges, the Exchequer, the Justices of Jewry, or other appropriate officers for possible administrative action. Petitions of a more general character were reserved to the king and Council. Relief granted to these general petitions resulted in statutes, a word derived from the Latin *statutum*, meaning "it is decided." At this point in constitutional development, petitions were not drafted in the form of a bill ultimately to be adopted, but in general terms. The form of relief, if any, was determined solely by the king and Council.

Commons now saw a simple means of increasing its power. It began to refuse to make financial grants until the king had redressed its grievances. By the fifteenth century, Commons was sufficiently powerful to require that the statute be written out in final form before it granted financial aid; but only after 1500 did the modern period of parliamentary action begin with Commons' drafting its own bills.

The English practice was part of the legal inheritance of the American colonies, and the legacy shows signs of becoming more rather than less important. In the nineteenth century, moreover, a movement began which further enhanced the position of legislation. It was the movement toward codification.

Codification

Legislation can take many forms. In the dawn of a legislative era, statutes take the form of a reproduction of existing custom. This, for example, was the major content of the Anglo-Saxon dooms and of the Twelve Tables of the Romans. In more developed legal systems, statutes can, as they generally do in this country, take the form of piecemeal legislation designed to solve particular problems in the law. Sometimes these are compiled in one way or another into sets of "codes," but this is not the meaning of the word as it will be used here.

A true code is a new creation that comes about during the maturity of a legal system. When a legal system has developed myriad concepts, principles, and rules, the legal profession sometimes molds them into a unified whole by resolving conflicts, setting forth basic principles, and, in general, consolidating the developments in law to that time.

Early codes. The first true code was that of Justinian in A.D. 534. It did these very things to Roman law, summarizing legal developments from the time of Cicero (106-43 B.C.) almost to its date. This code came after nearly a millennium of Roman legal history and succeeded an era of mere collections of legislation.

Modern codes probably find their genesis in the Prussian code directed by Frederick the Great (1712-1786). Although not adopted until eight years after his death, it was in effect until 1900. The French were also attracted to codification, and Napoleon's most lasting work was directing the development of the French Civil Code of 1804, which was a model for subsequent codes during the nineteenth century in two dozen countries, as well as the state of Louisiana and the province of Quebec. The later German Civil Code of 1900 was, in turn, the effective model for the modern codes of Japan, Switzerland, Brazil, China, and Greece.

In English law, codification was suggested by Francis Bacon in the early seventeenth century. Save for a few experiments in British India, however, these suggestions came to nothing.

The idea of codification took hold in the United States in the middle of the nineteenth century. Under the influence of its major proponent, David Dudley Field, codes in separate areas of the law were proposed in numerous states. Instead of one comprehensive code covering all law, the American movement took the form of attacks on five special areas: civil procedure, criminal procedure, civil law, criminal law, and politics. Field's code of civil procedure was the most successful, perhaps because it was the most needed. It was enacted first in New York in 1850 and later adopted in about thirty other states. Civil procedure, encumbered with the archaisms and anachronisms of English procedure, was in need of total overhaul, not just fragmentary reform. Field's code of criminal procedure met with less success. Only four states adopted all five codes.

Uniform acts. The form of codification which proved most adaptable to the Anglo-American legal climate was even narrower than Field's conception. Rather than to codify all of even the civil law, the route chosen was to codify particular parts. New York, for instance, codified its real property law as early as 1828. Comprehensive penal codes were adopted by many of the states in the middle of the nineteenth century.

The American Bar Association, formed in 1878, sought to eliminate differences in law among the states. Particularly in the area of commercial law did such differences appear to be ridiculous, but when it became clear that federal legislation would be impolitic since a Constitutional amendment would be necessary, the association turned to the idea of uniform laws to be adopted by each state legislature. The thought was that a common statute would lead to uniform law.

A committee was formed to look into the feasibility of such enactments, and after two years, a number of states cooperated to form the National

Conference of Commissioners on Uniform State Laws. This group proposed a number of such acts including the Negotiable Instruments Act (1896), the Uniform Warehouse Receipts Act (1906), the Uniform Sales Act (1906), the Uniform Stock Transfer Act (1909), the Uniform Partnership Act (1914), and the Uniform Conditional Sales Act (1918). The idea behind the uniform acts was dual: (1) to bring the law into line with current commercial practices and (2) to provide a single law which, if passed by each state in the same form, would lead to uniformity among the various states. These acts and others in the area of commercial law were widely adopted.

But the hopes of the drafters of the uniform acts were defeated in two ways. It is perhaps unfortunate, but also unavoidable, that each state exercised its power to interpret the acts as it saw fit. It was neither unfortunate nor avoidable, however, that commercial practices changed over a period of fifty years, creating the need for new statutes by the 1940's. Instead of proposing new, separate acts, the drafters decided to combine cognate acts into one large statute.

The American Law Institute and the National Conference of Commissioners on Uniform State Laws joined to produce a new Uniform Commercial Code—an integrated statute combining eight previously separate areas. The first draft appeared in 1952 and was adopted by Pennsylvania in 1954. Further changes were made in 1957 and 1958, and by 1963 the Uniform Commercial Code was law, or shortly to become law, in more than a quarter of the states.

Conclusion

The Anglo-American legal system has resisted the lure of out-and-out codification but has applied the principle of codification to areas in which it is practically and politically feasible. Even in these areas, however, legal analysis proceeds along traditional Anglo-American lines and does not follow the civil-law approach. The doctrine of precedent rules in the interpretation of these codes, even in the few states which have virtually complete codification. There is also a tendency on the part of lawyers and judges to treat codes as mere declarations of what the law would be in the absence of the code and, sometimes, even to ignore the codes.

In most of our states most of the law is still common law and can be ascertained only by going back to past cases. The extent to which codification will continue to advance is not a matter for safe prognostication, but it appears that the basic modes of legal analysis in the Anglo-American legal system will not change appreciably in the foreseeable future.

Doctrinal writings

ALTHOUGH NEVER SO IMPORTANT AS IN the civil law, doctrinal writings hold an important place as a secondary source of law in the Anglo-American legal system. For the very earliest periods, indeed, they are equivalent to true law, for there are no other sources.

Overt legal writing began in England in the reign of Henry I (1100-1135), when several attempts were made to restate the Anglo-Saxon laws in the light of Norman changes. Prime among them, and perhaps the earliest true law book after the Conquest, is a volume known as the *Laws of Henry (Leges Henrici)*. Its name is unfortunate, because it derives from the first part of the book which is a reproduction of the Charter of Henry I given at his coronation. The bulk of the book is an attempt to bring the laws of Edward the Confessor up to date.

In the same reign, another book, *Laws of Edward the Confessor,* was compiled by an unknown author. It purported to be a collection of laws in force in England at the time of the Conquest, ascertained by William through jury inquests. Its true nature as a forgery was not discovered until the nineteenth century, after it had influenced writers such as Bracton and Coke, who took what it said as the truth.

From Glanvill to Littleton

If he were in Washington today, Henry II might be a controversial, vigorous government official. His emotional instability either accounted for, or did not hinder, his great drive, his talent as an administrator and legislator, and his desire to replace the chaos of Stephen's reign with order and to strengthen the central government. During his reign, a *responsalis* could appear for a litigant and direct the procedural aspects of his case, the possessory assizes were created, and legislation stirred with new life.

As a twelfth century administrator, Henry needed records of the emerging common-law system, particularly the most highly developed aspect of it, the Exchequer. When Richard Fitz Neal had been Henry's treasurer for some twenty years, he produced his *Dialogue of the Exchequer,* a basic source of information on early English fiscal matters, but not essentially a law book.

In or about 1187 a treatise appeared which has been attributed to Ranulph de Glanvill, one of Henry's favorites, soon to become his Chief Justiciar. This book was concerned solely with the law as administered in the king's courts. Its importance lay in its manner of organization as much as in the information it gave, for it set the style of legal writing for centuries in the future. At that time there were about fifty royal writs, and this volume was a commentary on them.

The next great book on the common law was Bracton's unfinished treatise of 1256. It, too, was a commentary on the writs, which by that time numbered about two hundred and fifty. Bracton's work was much more inclusive than the earlier one, and in some places he appears to have inserted civil-law concepts in order to fill the gaps in the still incomplete English law.

Bracton's work was important at two critical times. When it was written, its influence was immense, because it was the only authoritative statement of English law in existence. Second, and equally important, was the occasion of its re-publication in 1569, when his emphasis on royal responsibility was a needed counterinfluence to the prerogative powers then being demanded and exercised by the monarch. Lord Coke drew upon Bracton's influence and antiquity in his famous conflicts with the Crown, particularly in invoking his famous statement, "The King is King under God and the law." In the time of Bracton, of course, concepts of divine right in the king were still unknown, and the reaffirmation of Bracton's statement at a time when such claims were being made had a salutary effect.

Two much smaller books, modeled after their predecessors, appeared around 1290-1292. One is called *Fleta* and the second *Britton.* They represent the end of the first era in legal writing and illustrate the beginning of the use of French rather than Latin as the written language of the law. The year 1290 also saw the apocryphal *Mirror of Justices,* which purported to be a description of then current law in the light of the laws of King Alfred. This book, like the *Laws of Edward the Confessor,* is mentioned only because later ages placed much reliance upon it, despite its utter unreliability, until its false nature was revealed by late eighteenth century research.

From Littleton to Kent and Story

Perhaps in 1481, or only a half-dozen years after the introduction of printing in England, appeared the first edition of Thomas de Littleton's *Tenures*. Its subject, land law, was one with which the author, as a Common Pleas judge, was closely familiar. The book initiated a new trend in legal writing: organizing a text on a particular subject, not in the form of a commentary on writs but by subject, divided into chapters. After almost a century and a half of use, it was brought up to date and translated from its original law French by Lord Coke in 1628.[1] Various editions of *Coke on Littleton* were produced by later editors, adding modern annotations to the prior writings. The work was actively used in the United States until the beginning of the nineteenth century.

Contemporaneously, a new type of comparative law treatise appeared in Sir John Fortescue's *In Praise of the Laws of England*, about 1470. It was a comparative study of English and French law, presumably prepared for the instruction of Prince Edward. Around 1523 this was followed by a philosophical rationale of equity jurisprudence in the *Dialogues between a Doctor of Divinity and a Student of the Common Law* by Christopher St. Germain.

Lord Coke himself wrote the next monumental treatise on English law. The first of his four *Institutes* was the commentary on Littleton, the only one published before his death. His second *Institute* (1642) was a commentary on statutory law; the third (1644) a commentary on criminal law, and the fourth (1644) a history of the courts.

The seventeenth century saw various minor but important legal treatises, some of a practical nature and others concerned with general matters, particularly legal history. Two of the practical works involved the law merchant and are important because their dates are separated by rapid progress in the development of the law of negotiable instruments, which is reflected in them. The first is the *Constitution of the Law Merchant* by Gerard Malynes (1622); the second is John Marius' *Advice Concerning Bils of Exchange* (1651). Historical works include John Selden's *Table Talk* and Sir Matthew Hale's *History of the Common Law* and *History of Pleas of the Crown*.

In 1765 appeared the book that was to constitute a major text for American lawyers until the twentieth century—Blackstone's *Commentaries on the Laws of England*. Blackstone's commentaries were developed from a series of his lectures to college students, not prospective lawyers, when he was Vinerian Professor of English Law at Oxford University. His views are stated with clarity in his introduction.

> For I think it an undeniable position, that a competent knowledge of the laws of that society in which we live, is the proper accomplishment of

---

[1] English legal language is a composite of Latin, French, and English. Latin was the formal language of court documents until 1731; French was the language spoken in the courts until 1362 and did not disappear as the language of legal literature until the sixteenth century.

every gentleman and scholar; a highly useful, I had almost said essential, part of liberal and polite education. And in this I am warranted by the example of ancient Rome; where, as Cicero informs us, the very boys were obliged to learn the twelve tables by heart, as a *carmen necessarium* or indispensable lesson, to imprint on their tender minds an early knowledge of the laws and constitution of their country.[2]

The concept of a university chair devoted to law bore fruit in the United States in the Dane Professorship at Harvard Law School. The first occupant of that chair, Joseph Story, was also the author of a celebrated series of *Commentaries* in the 1820's.

From Kent and Story to the present day

Contemporary with Story's *Commentaries* were those of James Kent, law teacher, judge, and chancellor. While Kent's *Commentaries* were in the tradition of Blackstone's, Story's works are the first legal textbooks. Just as the alphabetically organized discussion of legal procedure, called an abridgment, was followed by an organized discussion of the legal system in the commentary, so the commentary was followed by a reasoned treatment of a particular branch of the law, which is called a textbook.[3]

After Story, authors followed the trend toward specialization foreshadowed centuries earlier by Littleton and given its modern impetus by Story. Today we have, for instance, treatises such as *Wigmore on Evidence, Williston on Contracts, Prosser on Torts,* and the like. The influence of these men is often so great that they have cast the line of development of the law in many areas. Their contribution is reduction of the mass of the common law, as found in myriad cases, to almost manageable proportions.

One modern and novel experiment in doctrinal writing is the Restatement movement sponsored by the American Law Institute, which was formed in 1923. The Restatement idea was to have a group of learned lawyers, judges, and law professors agree on the essence of the law in particular areas through research and discussion. One scholar was made responsible for the original draft of each topic, on which the others commented until a consensus was obtained. In this way, it was thought, individual personalities and ideas could be submerged in the thinking of the group.

A series of Restatements was produced, including those on contracts, agency, torts, and restitution. The effect of each on the law has differed, because some of them are deemed excellent by the profession, and others are not so highly regarded. The Restatements have not altered the traditional approach of the profession to legal analysis; their publication has meant only the addition of another reputable book in each area covered.

---

[2] 1 *Blackstone* 5-6. (The first number indicates the volume of the collection; the second indicates the page on which the reference is found.)

[3] Andrew Johnson, "The Influences of Nathan Dane on Legal Literature," 7 *Am. J. Legal Hist.* 28 (1963).

Courts and lawyers cite the Restatements, but the primary source of law is still the body of cases and statutes.

The law schools of this country produce considerable legal writing in their law reviews. Virtually all law schools publish journals, usually staffed by senior students. Eminent lawyers, judges, and law professors write the lead articles, and students comment on topics and cases of interest. For close analysis, the law reviews are probably more valuable than any other secondary legal source.

❧ PART III

The Common Law in Action

Real property

THE CONCEPT OF A FEE IS BASIC IN REAL property. The word "fee" is derived from the Latin *feodum,* meaning a fief, or feudal estate. As used in the law, a fee is an eternal interest in property. This in itself is an enigma, for the fact is that no one lives forever. The eternal-interest theory can be understood only by considering its consequences. If one has a fee, he can sell land so that the buyer may retain it after the seller's death; he can will it to his heirs, and he can divide it in time into any number of successive tenancies. The idea of absolute and eternal ownership of land did not come into existence until our legal system was relatively mature.

The Anglo-Saxon background. The Anglo-Saxons did not know the fee. Although the details are not clear, it seems that they held land in one of three ways. By far the most common was folkland. At one time it was thought that this was a system of common ownership, and that inhabitants of the vill annually distributed available tillable land. This was referred to as the mark system. Since the researches of Vinogradoff, a pioneer historian of early English law who wrote at the turn of the century, however, this theory has been abandoned. The truth is more prosaic: folkland means only land held under general or customary law. Since everyone was familiar with it, no one bothered to write down its characteristics, and so its workings are unclear to modern scholars.

It appears conjecturally that the family, rather than the individual, was the unit of ownership. On death of the head of the family, control seems to have passed to the next head of the household. Since there was little trading in land, except in the area held by the Danes, the question of the right to transfer did not arise. There is some indication that when land was given to the Church, the approval of all possible heirs was obtained. That approval, however, may have been merely precautionary and not a legal requisite.

A common form for ownership of land by churches or great men was by formal charter or grant from the king and his witan. This was known as bookland. Bookland was not held in absolute ownership, but it carried rights over the land which continued to be held, at the lowest level, as folkland. To the peasants tilling the soil, a grant of land by book meant merely a change of masters. Since the holders of the book were not interested in doing the actual farming, land held by book was folkland to the actual occupants. Some rights granted by book were to hold court and to collect taxes; the only duties required were the *trinodas necessitas* of (1) rendering military service, (2) repairing bridges within the land, and (3) repairing its roads.

Bookland was governed by the terms of the grant. Sometimes the right to will such land was given, and even when it was not, the land could be inherited by heirs. Church land was held by the successors in office of the original grantee. The duration of the estate was controlled by the terms of the book, and if nothing else was said, it was good only for the life of the recipient, after which it reverted to the former owner.

Laen land, the third type, was held for from one to three generations of the superior holder, with the occupier required to turn over to the superior certain quantities of produce. It resembled a modern lease rather than a sharecropping arrangement, except that crops were paid instead of a money rent. It usually was a written arrangement.

This device was widespread because it was one of the few ways to make a profit. Trade was by barter or by professional merchants at the fairs. Interest on the use of money was absolutely forbidden by church and lay law. By acquiring laen land, however, the tenant was entitled to the fruit of the land on payment of the annual dues. For the superior lord (usually a church), the advantage was a steady return from the land for approximately a century. Of course, by the end of three generations, the family holding the tenancy had become so accustomed to it that they considered it family property. It appears that the grantors of laen land occasionally settled the matter with the heirs of the last tenant by a regrant.

The Norman background. The feudal system as introduced by the Normans made important changes. William the Conqueror claimed that all the land in England was his and that anyone who held land held it either directly or indirectly of him. Holding directly from the king were the tenants in chief, and below them, in steps, were various lesser lords.

The highest type of ownership was military tenure, called knight's service. Feudalism was, in its inception, a military system: its purpose was to form, by a series of personal relationships, a military machine capable of immediate defense of the realm against external attack and internal revolt. The royal purse, however, was too slim to support a standing force, so land was used as a substitute.

In return for his land, the military tenant swore "to become your man for the tenement I hold of you and to bear faith to you of life and members and earthly honor against all other men." The details, however, were more involved. The vassal was to give the king the services of a number of knights for forty days in the year. Their number varied with the amount of land; their service was perpetual. If the vassal failed to deliver the knights, the land was to go back to the king.

This mode of raising an armed force may have been sufficient for a short expedition; but for permanent defense, a standing army was much preferable. During the twelfth century, actual service of knights was remitted in favor of a money payment called scutage, or *escuage,* and so it remained until the abolition of feudalism in 1660. Scutage was a fixed sum vulnerable to inflation, which appears to be part of the historical process that after a time made it all but worthless. It fact, although not in theory, it appears to have disappeared after 1384, and thereafter armies were raised with funds provided by parliamentary grant. This, as we have seen, was one of the causes of the addition of the House of Commons to Parliament. When feudalism was abolished in 1660, scutage was replaced by a tax on beer. So came a noble institution to a prosaic end.

The theory of knight's service created a real problem on the death of a vassal. Since knight's service was a personal relationship based on the mutual faithfulness of landlord and tenant, must the lord accept the heir of the tenant as the tenant's successor? The son might be an enemy of the lord, or unfaithful, or of doubtful courage. In feudal theory, the lord had a right to choose his vassal. This problem, too, came to be solved by money. On payment of a sum called relief, the regrant to the heir of the vassal became a matter of right, once the heir had taken an oath of homage or fealty to the lord. Relief also became a fixed sum with diminishing value.

A similar feudal problem was created when the daughter of a vassal married. Suppose she married an enemy of the vassal's lord? This was unthinkable. The marriage must be approved by the lord. But this, too, did not occur without the passing of money, for the hand of the daughter of a landed gentleman was valuable. Marriage to such a woman brought prestige, land, and valuable gifts. Subsequently, and with little warrant even in feudal theory, this right of the marriage fee extended to the marriage of a vassal's son as well.

A further problem arose. Suppose that on the death of the vassal, his son was not of age. The problem could not have been infrequent in those days of short life expectancy. Who should take care of the child? A relative might find it more profitable to kill him than to maintain him, for the relative might inherit the estate. The relative might be an enemy of the lord. The lord, therefore, had the right of wardship; and in return for keeping the ward and educating him in appropriate skills, he had the right to use the child's land until he attained the age of majority without accounting in any way for its profits. This right, like the right of marriage, remained valuable for centuries.

The lord also had the right of aid from his tenant. Financial emergencies were posed by the marriage of his eldest daughter and the knighting of his eldest son (both of which required the giving of gifts and parties) or by his capture and consequent need for ransom money. By the thirteenth century, both the amount of aid and the occasions on which it could be demanded were fixed.

Last, there was the right of escheat. If the tenant was convicted of a felony other than treason, the land, after the profits were taken by the king for a year and a day, escheated to the lord. If the crime was treason, the land was totally forfeited to the king, and the lord lost all his rights even though it was his vassal who had committed the crime.

Another type of tenancy was the sergeanty. Sergeant means servant, and these tenants had particular services to perform, either military or nonmilitary in nature. A tenant in sergeanty might have had duties, for instance, as a chamberlain, an armoror, a cook, or an esquire. Under early feudalism any lord could create a subordinate sergeanty, but by the fifteenth century sergeanties were held only of the king.

Sergeanty is another example of feudal expediency. Not having the hard cash to pay sergeants, the king obtained their services by giving them land. Prestige attended the vassal's position: relief and aids applied to all sergeanties, and the presence of the rights of wardship and marriage indicated a grand, rather than a petty, sergeanty.

Churches held land in frankalmoign tenure, also called free alms. The church was to perform spiritual services such as the saying of masses for the donor. Obviously, neither relief, wardship, nor marriage could apply to these estates.

Socage tenure was the least of the freehold estates (those protected in the royal courts). It required an oath of faithfulness, but no military service. In fact, no real services may have been due at all, and only a purely formal obligation, such as the giving of one red rose at midsummer to signify the relationship, may have been required. Some sokemen gave a yearly payment, and others gave personal service such as plowing the lord's land. This latter obligation, however, was not on call, as in villein tenure, but due only at specified times.

For a time, each tenant could create a subtenant under him in one of these relationships. A tenant in chief, for instance, holding by military tenure, might give part of his land to another military tenant and part to a church. The prime tenancy, however, remained responsible for the feudal dues and services to the king.

The medieval tenures were, therefore, characterized by a personal relationship between lord (landlord) and man (tenant) which was, theoretically, to last only for the lifetime of the tenant. In fact, however, on payment of relief and the giving of homage, a tenancy could descend to heirs.

Inheritance of land. One further preliminary matter remains, and that is primogeniture, the rule that land descends to the eldest son. At the time of the Conquest, primogeniture was known and applied in some places on the Continent, but was not followed in England. The dominant scheme of inheritance was parage.

In parage, the land descended to all the male heirs of the tenant, subject to the lord's right to approve or disapprove the heirs. The eldest son was responsible for the feudal dues and services on behalf of the group, but his brothers were equal to him. Parage avoided splitting the land among the heirs, which, from the feudal point of view, was undesirable: as the process continued, each son might become the holder of a piece of land insufficient to support the feudal dues and services he owed. From an economic point of view, splitting the land would be equally disastrous, for a rich, prolific family might disintegrate into a group of impoverished peasants in the course of a few generations.

The concept of primogeniture probably arose out of the procedure for selecting a new king. On the Continent, kingship was hereditary and descended to the oldest son. With the Normans, the idea of hereditary kingship came to England and was soon applied to military tenures. Then, apparently for economic reasons, primogeniture was applied to villein tenures (the holdings of peasants on the manors). Socage was the last tenure to come under primogeniture, and probably did so purely by example. Primogeniture, like parage, achieved the feudal purpose of keeping the landholdings intact.

Certain areas in England retained old customs. Kent continued parage under the name of gavelkind, while in other areas a custom called borough English gave the land to the youngest son. In all places, however, parage was the rule when only female heirs were left. In this application it was known as coparceny.

Alienation of land. The term "alienation" means, literally, getting rid of something. One may get rid of land by selling it for money, trading it for other land or goods, or by giving it away. It is a voluntary act during life; one cannot alienate land after death.

The scope and power of alienation before primogeniture is not clear. In Anglo-Saxon times it appears that bookland, at least, could be alienated without the consent of the heirs. Norman charters, however, both on the Continent and in England, reveal a propensity toward obtaining the joinder or consent of all heirs—not only sons, but daughters and other relatives who might, by chance, come into the estate on the death of the owner. Around the year 1200, a swift and mysterious change took place. Glanvill's writings, around 1186, reveal that the old system of approvals still existed, but it had totally disappeared by 1256, the time of Bracton.

The change may have been caused by the introduction of primogeniture and legally facilitated by the doctrine of warranty. Consents, it appears, were needed in order to assure equal division of the inheritance among the sons. Otherwise a father might, by conveyance, prefer one son to another. Primogeniture eliminated this possibility. Furthermore, a father who conveyed land could warrant that he and his heirs would protect the title against attack. The warranty would bind the son, who therefore was unable to regain the land from the purchaser.

It is clear from other evidence that royal judges were highly in favor of free alienation of land, perhaps because of their realization, as the king's men, that free alienation loosened the feudal bonds in the ranks below the king and thus indirectly enhanced the power of the Crown.

Objections to alienation, under feudal theory, could come from the lord, a more potent source. The relationship between lord and tenant was personal; by what authority could the tenant put another person in his place without the lord's consent?

To unravel this problem we must first look at the two possible modes of alienation under feudalism. The first and simplest was substitution. Suppose T is the tenant of L. He might, conceivably, sell all his land to X and have X take his place as L's tenant. Or he might prefer to create a new subtenancy. In that case, L would still be the lord of T, and T would be the lord of X. This was called subinfeudation.

Under either method dues and services were still owed to L. If they were not rendered either by X, in the case of substitution, or T, in the case of subinfeudation, the land came back to the lord.

Both modes of alienation were disadvantageous to the lord. A poor man might be substituted for a wealthy man, a disloyal person for a loyal person, or an enemy for a friend. If a tenant subinfeudated another for a substantial money payment and reserved purely nominal services such as one red rose at midsummer, the value of the superior lord's rights plummeted. Suppose the tenant died. The lord still had the duty to care for the tenant's oldest son, but now, instead of being permitted to use the tenant's land until the son's majority without accounting for profit or waste, he received the one red rose per year. If the tenant committed a felony that resulted in escheat, again the lord received the nominal service. Or the tenant may have given the land to a church in return for its promise to say prayers for the repose of his soul. This promise was of no value to the lord.

A still more involved evasive practice took place. A tenant might convey land to a church with the understanding that the church would subinfeudate him for lesser services. The result was that the superior lord now had the church for a tenant, with the resulting loss of feudal dues, but the erstwhile tenant still had the benefit of the land with his obligations considerably reduced. The church now stood as an intermediate tenant between the superior lord and the tenant.

Protests were made against all these practices. The 1217 edition of Magna Carta spoke out against them, the Petition of Barons presented to the King at Oxford in 1258 requested a remedy for unauthorized gifts by their tenants to clerics, and the Provisions of Westminster in 1259 purported to give them a remedy, but was ineffectual.

On the Continent, the lord's consent to alienation appears to have been the established practice, but perhaps in a newly conquered country where the lands of all enemy English lords were forfeited, it was expected that subinfeudation would be used as the primary means of filling the feudal ranks. So long as subinfeudation (for this was the normal mode of alienation) was not abused, objections were not effective.

Only in 1279, with the Statute of Mortmain, was the practice of giving lands to churches even impeded. Thenceforth, gifts to churches were to be made only by express license from the king, obtained on payment of a fee. These licenses, however, were freely granted.

During the thirteenth century, it became increasingly clear that tenants in chief of the king could not alienate their lands without royal consent. While lesser lords who were prejudiced in their rights could, in turn, alienate to the injury of their own lords, only the king was no man's tenant. Therefore the ultimate effect of the practice fell on him. This he would not permit.

The 1290 statute *Quia Emptores Terrarum* (because purchasers of land) finally stopped the practice of subinfeudation among even lesser lords. It forbade subinfeudations of fee simple estates. A tenant in fee could still subinfeudate, however, by granting an estate less than a fee, such as a life estate or an estate in tail. The statute permitted free alienation of part of the estate by substitution if the services due the superior lord were apportioned according to the quantities of land remaining in the parties' hands. The statute did not apply to lands held directly of the king, and therefore tenants in chief could not alienate in any manner without the king's consent.

Abolition of subinfeudation could have been popular only with the king and the tenants in chief, for the king had no dues to avoid, and the tenants in chief, by that date, could not avoid them. Yet the statute was a good compromise. The lord's rights could not be diminished, and yet the tenant could alienate land. A mode of avoiding feudal dues was thereby abolished.

The statute may have been beneficial in a more subtle way. The abolition of subinfeudation in fee simple estates tended to limit the number of rungs in the feudal ladder reaching down from the king to the actual tenant in demesne. This was a political benefit in that it kept down the number of lords and barons, so that those who remained were closer to the royal government. Natural processes of extinction of lines and escheat of estates to the immediately superior lords assisted this process.

The uses of a fee

The rights of the heir to inherit land and of the owner to sell it are two essential elements of the fee interest. If land were not inheritable, the most one could convey would be an estate for the duration of his own life, for that is all he would own. If land were inheritable but could not be sold, its value would be considerably reduced, for value consists, at least in part, of what one can expect a sale to bring.

A fee owned by one person is called a fee simple. When owned with another person it may be a tenancy in common, a joint tenancy, a coparceny, or a tenancy by the entireties, depending on the relationship between the owners and the incidents of ownership.

A tenancy in common is ownership by more than one individual in which shares need not be equal, and in which each owner has full control to sell, encumber, or will his individual portion. A joint tenancy is a second form of multiple ownership in which the shares must be equal and derived from the same conveyance, and in which each party may sell his own portion (thus converting it into a tenancy in common between the new party and the old), or he may encumber it, but he cannot will it. On death, the decedent's portion is divided equally among the remaining owners. Coparceny, long obsolete, is the equal interest inherited by daughters when, under the scheme of primogeniture, there was no male heir. A tenancy by the entireties is ownership of land by husband and wife, and neither can sell, encumber, or will his interest.

The life estate. Since a fee is eternal ownership, an owner of a fee can divide it temporally into successive interests. He may, for instance, convey the land to another for the duration of that other person's life. It should be noticed that a life estate may, in actuality, be shorter than a lease for years, such as one for fifty years. But in contemplation of law any estate for life is more important than any for a term of years. A term of years is not a freehold.

There is a variation of the life estate known as the estate *pur autre vie,* or estate for the life of another. Suppose, for instance, that A has an estate for his life and grants it to B. On the valid principle that A cannot grant more than he has, B gets what A had, which is an estate for the duration of A's life.

By definition, a life estate always has a fee above it. It is implied that on the death of the life tenant, the land will revert to the owner of the fee or to his heirs. Also, any number of life estates can be carved out of a fee. For instance: A, an owner in fee, may provide B with a life estate which is to go to C on B's death, to D on C's death, and so on.

The life estate was so common in the early days of our law that it was presumed to be granted merely by the statement that the land was conveyed "to A." A fee could be created only by the words "to A and his heirs." The magic words "and his heirs" remained essential until very recent times in order to create a fee in the common-law jurisdictions of the United States.

The estate in fee tail. Following a long period of development, the details of which are not absolutely clear, the provisions of the Statute of Westminster II known as *De Donis Conditionalibus* (1285) created the estate in fee tail. The origin of the device apparently lay in the desire of parents to assist a young couple in the founding and perpetuation of a family, but it became a method of perpetuating a family's feudal status.

The estate in tail, or entail, restricted ownership of land to a particular family line. If the line ever (in theory at least) became extinct, the land was to revert to the original grantor's line. The form of the grant was, for instance, "to A and the heirs of his body." This was called a tenancy in tail general. As Lord Coke translated from Littleton:

> Tenant in taile generall is, where lands or tenements are given to a man, and to his heires of his bodie begotton. In this case it is said generall taile, because whatsoever woman, that such tenant taketh to wife, (if he

hath many wives, and by every of them hath issue) yet everie one of these issues by possibilitie may inherit the tenements by force of the gift; because that everie such issue is of his bodie ingendred.[1]

Such an estate could also be given to a woman and the heirs of her body by whatever husband.

On the other hand, "Tenant in taile speciall is, where lands or tenements are given to a man and to his wife, and to the heires of their two bodies begotton. In this case none shall inherit by force of this gift, but those that be engendred between them two." [2] If the grantee was a daughter or female cousin of the grantor, a statement that the conveyance was in "frankmarriage" was sufficient to accomplish the same object.

Other variations were possible: an estate tail male, restricted to males in the line (if these lapsed, the estate reverted to the donor's line); an estate tail female, restricting it to the female line; an estate tail special male, in which the estate went only to the male heirs of a given married couple, and so forth.

A major question for two centuries was whether the estate tail ever changed into a fee simple. As a fee tail, it could not effectively be sold; but as a fee simple, it could be sold. In the fourteenth and fifteenth centuries it appeared that the estate tail would ripen into a fee after three generations in the family (recalling the pre-1285 conditional fee), but by the end of the fifteenth century it appeared that an estate tail continued until the extinction of the blood line.

The device was valuable to the heirs of the tenant in tail. Their estate was protected from alienation by sale or (until 1540) by lease. They were not responsible for the debts or incumbrances of the tenant in tail unless he went bankrupt after 1654, when a statute permitted sale of their interests to pay his debts. Until 1534, heirs of tenants in tail did not lose their estates due to forfeitures to the king arising from treasonable activity, but their estates were still protected from escheat to their lords due to their ancestors' simple felonies.[3]

By the early sixteenth century the device of the common recovery had developed. This made it possible for the tenant in fee tail, in many cases, to convey a fee simple estate to a third party. The common recovery was a completely fictitious suit—a pious fraud. The device went through many stages, but the simplest example is the single voucher. Suppose, for instance, that A was in possession as a tenant in fee tail and desired to convey a fee to B. B would sue him for the land, alleging that A had no legal title to it and that it really was owned by B. A would enter an appearance and call upon X (from whom, he alleged quite fictitiously, he had purchased the land) to defend the title in accordance with the warranty given by X to A. This process was called vouching to warranty. X was called the common vouchee, because he usually was the court crier and frequently acted in this capacity. X would appear but would subse-

---

[1] *Coke on Littleton,* Book 1, sections 14, 15.
[2] *Id.* at section 16.
[3] 4 Blackstone, *Commentaries* 385.

quently default, whereupon judgment would be given to the plaintiff, B, against A, and the court would give another judgment to A against X, presumably for lands of equal value, because of X's breach of warranty in defaulting. X, of course, was without resources and was not expected to give A anything. The suit resulted in the conveyance of a fee estate to B. This device could also be used, in a more complicated form, to extinguish or bar the entail without a sale.

The combination of the rule that an estate in fee tail could not be sold, encumbered, or escheated to the detriment of the heirs, coupled with the practical fact that it could be converted into a fee by the device of the common recovery, made it a most valuable form of ownership. It could be a bulwark against disaster, a relatively untouchable asset, and at the same time perfectly marketable.

Reversions and remainders. In any type of conveyance, if the owner did not dispose of the complete fee, he necessarily retained a reversion. If he gave a tenancy for one year, the rest of the infinity of time was his in reversion. If he gave a life estate, the fee reverted to him or his heirs at the death of the life tenant. Seisin, which refers to possession as applied to land, and the duty to perform the feudal dues and services were in the reversioner. When an estate in fee tail was granted and the line became extinct, there was a reversion to the line of the original grantor—technically called a possibility of reverter. Seisin was in the tenant in tail. A reversionary interest must be distinguished, however, from escheat. Escheat gave the land to the superior lord on the death of a tenant in fee who died without any heirs, either lineal or collateral.

A remainder was the equivalent concept when the infinity of time left after the granting of a lesser estate was in the hands of someone other than the donor. If A gave a life estate to B, with a remainder to C and his heirs, A rid himself of all his interest in that land. There was nothing left to revert to him. B had a life estate which, as the first estate to come into enjoyment, was called the particular estate. C had the remainder— all that was left over after B's life estate determined (ended). It was a vested remainder because it was not subject to any condition other than the death of B (which was sure to happen); and if C was also dead at the time of B's death, his heirs took the fee in his stead. If he had no heirs, the estate would escheat. Seisin and the duty to perform feudal obligations were in the remainderman.

A contingent remainder, on the other hand (1) goes to a person or persons whose identity is uncertain at the time of the grant, or (2) is to come into being after the happening of an uncertain event in the future.

An example of the first type is a grant to A for life, with a remainder to the heirs of B. Since no man can have an heir until he is dead, the recipients of that estate in remainder are not known, and a contingent remainder is created. By the middle of the fifteenth century, the common law had worked out a solution to this type of contingency. If the condition was actually met by the time of the determination (ending) of the particular (first) estate, it was valid. If B was dead by the time of A's death, the defect was cured, and the heirs of B (who were then known) took a fee. If he was not dead, the land reverted to the original grantor.

An example of the second type is a grant to A for life and, in case B survives him, to B and his heirs. Here the recipient of the remainder is certainly B, but B will not take this estate unless he survives A, and this is an uncertain future event. Again, since this estate of B depended on the death of a living person, it would be cured if B actually survived A.

But who had seisin? Generally, in contingent remainders, seisin was held to be in the life tenant until his death. This, of course, meant that the estate might be destroyed by escheat or forfeiture if the holder of the life estate committed treason or felony or if he conveyed the land before the contingency occurred.

Whether the contingency could be something other than the death of the holder of the life estate was long a puzzle to the common law. Various rules concerning "repugnant" conditions arose when these matters came before the courts in the sixteenth century and thereafter, all subject to numerous refinements and uncertainties. Such remainders were finally protected by creating trusts to hold them until the occurrence of the contingency.

The modern rules on remainders protect both vested and contingent remainders of all legal types, and the basic problem is to make certain that the time in which they will ultimately vest, or become certain, is not outside the legal limit. For this an admirably involved rule known as the Rule Against Perpetuities was developed out of the *Duke of Norfolk's* case (1682). Basically, its object is that all estates are to vest at a date not later than twenty-one years after the end of a life (or the last of several lives) in being at the time of the creation of the estate.

Conclusion. These illustrations of the life estate, estate in tail, and vested and contingent remainders are merely a few examples of the uses to which the concept of the fee, the eternal interest in land, might be put. Others include such esoteric matters as estates subject to conditions subsequent, conditions precedent, implied (unexpressed) reversions, rights of entry, and possibilities of reverter. These devices are by no means antiquities, but today they are basically the subject matter of that branch of equity known as the law of trusts, for future interests in purely legal estates are rare indeed.

Wills of land

Two sticks of the bundle called ownership—alienation and inheritance—having been examined, consider now a third: the right to devise land by wills.

The matter must begin with a distinction between succession and testamentary distribution. Succession is a scheme, customary or legislative, for the devolution of a deceased person's property. It prescribes one's heirs. A testament is a voluntary provision for the disposition of one's property at death. A modern will or testament is, by definition, revocable until the moment of death. In succession, the law designates one's heirs, but a testator makes his own heirs.

Roman law. In early Roman law, all legal rights over property were vested in the family, not in individuals; but they were exercised by the father, who was also responsible for family worship. There were no testaments, and succession was controlled by custom. On the death of the father, not only control of family property but also the personality and position of the father devolved upon his successors. The first in line of succession were those who were in his legal power during his lifetime. On his death they became *sui juris,* or independent. If there were no successors, adopted or natural, succession passed to the *agnati,* or those descended from a common male ancestor. In the absence of *agnati* it went to the *gens,* or clan, which was a group claiming a common remote ancestor, either actual or mythical.

The fear that all these might fail and that there would be no one to tend one's grave, to the great torment of his spirit, brought about the device of adoption, which resembled a will only in that it was a voluntary act. The next step was provision for a public declaration of the person to become the heir. This was followed, in turn, by an adaptation of the early Roman sale of property: the *patrimonium* (all the powers of the father over property, family, and worship) was transferred in the presence of a public official to a third person who was to distribute it after the father's death in accordance with the father's express wishes. Subsequently, under the praetors, a written document, or testament, was permitted.

This process accompanied the general individualization of property. The transition from family ownership to individual control and ownership took place as Roman society gradually changed from a small, closely knit group to an enormous trading and commercial society in which family ownership had to cease.

Anglo-Saxon "wills." The power to dispose of land at death was, it appears, in the hands of only great men in Anglo-Saxon times, and then only with royal approval. The concept was of a gift, to take effect at death (*post obit* gift). It was not a will in the modern sense, because it was not revocable. Normally a written document, it had neither a settled form nor a settled theory. The donee often was a church.

Those of lesser rank could make a deathbed disposition of personal property before witnesses and thus divide their chattels among the objects of their bounty. Only part of one's chattels could be disposed of in this way, however.

According to Maitland, these two devices merged before the Conquest into a document called the *cwide,* which apparently required the approval of the king to be effective. This always was used by great men only; lands of other people could be left by the *post obit* gift, and their chattels could be disposed of by the deathbed gift.

Norman wills. By the beginning of the thirteenth century, a rule against the willing of land was coming into being. Glanvill, in 1187, spoke out against deathbed dispositions of land on the ground that at such a time, when a person is perhaps in pain and definitely in dire peril, his judgment may be impaired to the detriment of his natural heirs. This, however, did not supply a reason for the rejection of a *post obit* gift of land, made while a person was still in good health. Nor does feudal theory provide a reason, for the *post obit* gift seems merely an alternative way of transferring land by substitution, an accepted practice. The reason probably was the desire of the royal courts to protect the natural heirs. If, indeed, the natural heir confirmed the *post obit* gift, there was no question as to its validity, although the underlying theory is not clear.

At a later date, another reason could be ascribed for the prohibition against wills of land. The doctrine of seisin, subsequently developed, required an actual physical transfer of possession of land, or of some token thereof, such as a twig or piece of turf, at a formal ceremony on the land or in sight of it, to make an effective transfer. This ceremony, known as livery of seisin, is impossible, of course, in a will of any type.

Despite the general restriction on wills of land in the royal courts, such was the force of custom that in certain boroughs, such as London, ancient rights to make wills of land remained effective.

Disposition of chattels effective at death, however, continued throughout England. Because of the connection of such gifts with deathbed distributions, the last rites of the Church, and gifts to the Church, the Church came to have jurisdiction over them. It developed the law concerning wills of personal property and executorships until the abolition of its jurisdiction over such matters after the Reformation, when control passed into the hands of Chancery.

Uses and wills. The concept of the use is simple. It merely requires that one person give property to another person or group of persons with the understanding that, as between them, the giver shall be the beneficial owner, while for all other purposes the recipient owns it. The recipient holds the property to the use of the giver or, as we would say today, in trust for the donor.

The roots of this device, to which analogies can be found in Roman law, lie earlier than our court records. There is reason to believe that it was used by the Crusaders, who conveyed lands to friends for their own convenience during their absence. Although one could not will land, he could instruct his friends concerning its disposition if he did not return from his holy venture. The common-law courts, to be sure, did not enforce this intention. At the earliest period, uses may have been enforced by the ecclesiastical courts, but by the reign of Henry III (1216-1272) the Courts Christian no longer had any jurisdiction over this arena of litigation. After that reign, enforcement lay only in the conscience of the friends or by the persuasion or authority of their confessors, since this obligation was recognized by the Church and was the subject of spiritual sanctions. Often, if not usually, uses were created by conveying the land to more than one person, so that each could watch the other. The use had other purposes, such as to avoid creditors' claims, to convey land to religious corporations until 1391 (after such conveyances were prohibited in 1279 by the Statute of Mortmain), and to avoid escheat and feudal revenues.

From the middle of the fifteenth century, uses were regularly enforced in Chancery, although the common-law courts refused to recognize them. As one consequence, while wills of land were technically impossible, an effective substitute for a will was available through the device of a use. The party to whom the land was entrusted could be directed to convey it to a certain person or to certain persons on the donor's death.

The year 1536 was crucial in the development of wills of land. In that year the Statute of Uses altered the use device in a way that made disposition of land at death impossible. Uses had been under attack by the king for some time. While some of its employments were valid and benign, others were fraudulent, and many deprived the king of revenue. Henry VIII, in order to regain his revenues and, perhaps incidentally, to halt fraudulent practices, determined to outlaw the use. The Statute of Uses provided that if A conveyed land to B to the use of C, the use in the hands of B was immediately destroyed, and full title to the land went to C. An attempt, therefore, to instruct B to convey the land to C upon A's death was not a substitute for a will, but a present conveyance.

Modern developments. By 1536 the use device had become so commonly employed by the growing mercantile class, in particular, that its abolition caused considerable consternation, for it ended the customary means of leaving land at death in accordance with one's desires. The resulting outcry was the efficient cause of the Statute of Wills (1540) that provided for wills of all socage tenancies and up to two-thirds of military tenures. Upon the abolition of feudalism in 1660, all land, of course, became subject to disposition by will.

With the coming of the Industrial Revolution and the corporate form of business in the nineteenth century, vast fortunes of previously unimaginable size came into existence—potent competitors to organized political government. Coupled with the need of government for more and more funds for its various assumed tasks, these fortunes led to a new approach to testamentary disposition of property. Although the right to make a will is undoubted, taxation of estates and inheritances has seriously hampered the transfer of economic power from one generation to another. Just as the income tax has become an accepted and admitted way to the redistribution of income during life, so death taxes have become a means of avoiding the concentration of economic power in particular families or groups. Our feudal forebears paid relief to obtain their inheritances; we, their successors, pay taxes.

Economic and social factors

What has been described here is the tortuous path taken by the law in its attempt to accommodate itself to changing economic and social conditions. At the beginning of the Norman period, the law tried to meet the needs of a society that was still, basically, on a war footing. Feudalism was the economic answer to the problems presented to a conquering population with widespread interests. Feudalism was also a political system for governing the nation and a social system for the people who, in its status arrangement, found prestige.

When, a century after the Conquest, the military needs of England became less pressing, the Crown had the opportunity to consolidate its power and advance its purposes. There resulted a proliferation of administration and the growth of professional branches in government, including the courts. The imposition of scutage and the creation of a standing army meant that the military reasons for feudalism no longer existed, but feudalism remained because, by that time, it was the basis for the political and social structure.

The next movement was toward increased commerce. Land had been the ultimate source of wealth, separating the impoverished from the well-to-do; but as commerce increased, other classes developed—the artisans and the bourgeoisie. Their wealth was envied by the Crown, and their financial aid was sought by admitting them into government through the House of Commons. Ultimately, pressures by these groups fashioned much of the law. By the seventeenth century they had destroyed feudalism, and the modern period began.

These changes in the law were all the more remarkable because they were accomplished with a minimum of legislation or revolution. Not only did the existence of the House of Commons make it possible for the political scheme to change by slight steps from time to time, but the nature and process of the common law permitted law to change as well. The independence of the judiciary was no small factor in this process, for it deemed itself, and proved itself, strong enough to defy royal authority.

Other parts of land-law development, particularly the transfer of villein tenancies to copyhold estates after the Black Death and the recognition accorded terms of years in land leases by the royal courts, are of considerable importance, but cannot be treated here. It may be sufficient to say that they also came about in response to economic and social changes and were quite independent of legislation.

Torts

9

IT IS PERHAPS UNFORTUNATE, BUT TRUE, that no universally acceptable definition of the word "tort" exists. In derivation, the word simply means a wrong. In practice it indicates some invasion or interference with a right of person, property, or reputation. In order to determine whether a tort exists, however, it is necessary to determine what legally protected rights of person, property, or reputation one has, which are not to be interfered with or invaded. Such a determination is the basis of the whole law of torts.

Torts today may be classified in terms of intent. Some torts are intentional, such as assault and battery. Others are the result of carelessness, or what the law calls negligence. In general, a negligent tort is the result of activity falling short of ordinary standards of care, as those standards are determined by the law. There is also a small area in the law of torts where liability is imposed regardless of intent or negligence—e.g., absolute liability.

These modern classifications, however, are scarcely a century old. They came into existence and developed with change and abolition of the old forms of action. The older law did not speak in terms of negligence and willfulness.

The ancient law

In tracing the early law of torts, we inevitably come up against the fact that there was once no differentiation between crimes and torts. Wrongs were first classified as felonies and things which were not felonies. If an offense resulted in death, dismemberment, escheat, or outlawry, or could be prosecuted by means of the private criminal prosecution known as an appeal of felony (where battle decided the guilt of the accused), it was a felony. If it did not fall in that area, it was one of a vast group of offenses referred to as trespasses or transgressions. Therefore, said Bracton, "Every felony is a trespass, though every trespass is not a felony."

In this vast group of trespasses, those offenses we would call misdemeanors and those we would call torts were mixed indiscriminately. All these offenses were subject to amercements, or fines, some payable to the Crown and others to the injured party.

Undoubtedly, many trespasses of a civil nature were redressed in the local and seignorial courts, but with these we have little concern, for they contributed nothing we can easily trace to the growth of our common law of torts.

The writ of trespass. One of the earliest writs in the royal courts, originally used in King's Bench, was the writ of trespass. Under this writ, misdemeanor and tort were, in actuality, still unseparated. The writ of trespass was based on the fact that the "peace of the king" had been broken. An early form of the writ, for instance, accused the defendant of having committed an assault and battery against the plaintiff and against the peace of the king. The last phrase gave the King's Court jurisdiction over the case, which was not a criminal case at that time because words of felony were not involved, and because the case did not arise by the procedure of indictment. It was a private action. If the plaintiff was successful in proving his case, he could recover damages for the assault and battery, and in the same action, the king could impose his fine.

This device of permitting private suit in King's Bench by alleging the breach of the king's peace, which was essential to that court's jurisdiction, first appeared around the year 1250 and developed rapidly during the latter half of the thirteenth century. It was a vast improvement over the old Anglo-Saxon *bot,* because it awarded damages fitting the particular case and not based on any set scale of compensation. It was advantageous to the plaintiffs, for they not only procured the relatively impartial justice of the king's judges, but also the great power of the king and his sheriffs to enforce the judgment that was rendered.

The nominate trespass actions. With the passage of time, the writ of trespass was divided into separate varieties which had specific names and therefore are referred to as the nominate, or named, actions. There was, for instance, the action previously mentioned concerning trespass to the person, called trespass *vi et armis* (with force and arms). Trespass to real property was called trespass *quare clausum fregit* (for breaching the close), and trespass to goods was called trespass *de bonis asportatis* (for taking the goods). The forms were strict, and for a case to be brought successfully, the facts alleged and proved had to come within the forms issued by Chancery. These writs provided remedies for the plaintiff only, and did not provide for a fine to the king.

The innominate trespass actions. Other actions of trespass arose which did not fit within the confines of a specific writ, but were framed to reflect the actual facts of a given case, and therefore varied from case to case. These were called the actions of trespass on the case. The phrase "on the case" merely indicates that the writs were not set forms, but reflected the true facts.

The circumstances that led to trespass on the case (often called case for short) are a matter of learned dispute centering about the true interpretation of Chapter 24 of the Statute of Westminster II (1285), which reads as follows:

> And whensoever from henceforth it shall fortune in the Chancery, that in one case a writ is found, and in like case falling under like law, and requiring like remedy, if found none, the clerks of the Chancery shall agree in making the writ, or shall adjourn the plaintiffs until the next parliament and write the cases in which they cannot agree, and refer them to the next parliament, and by consent of men learned in the law, a writ shall be made, lest it might happen hereafter that the court should long time fail to minister justice unto complainants.[1]

The statute was thought, for many years, to have created the authority in Chancery to issue writs of trespass on the case. The truth of the matter seems to be that after this statute, although not necessarily because of it, certain extensions of trespass started to appear. Sometimes writs of trespass issued by Chancery failed to include the magic words *vi et armis*, or to allege the breach of the king's peace which previously had been necessary to invoke the jurisdiction of the royal courts. Other extensions also appeared, such as writs that covered cases not involving a direct application of force (as was required in the nominate actions at that time) but alleging injury due to inaction or inattention to a voluntarily assumed duty or a duty imposed by law.

Theories of liability under the writs of trespass

The oldest of the nominate trespass actions rested on the theory of liability for (1) a willful act (2) causing direct injury. The court was not interested, from the point of view of liability, in what the plaintiff had suffered, but in what the defendant actually had done: there was no liability for not doing something.

If a case did not involve both willfulness and direct injury, the nominate actions would not lie. Suppose, for instance, that a defendant, intending to injure the plaintiff, broke the dam of his own pond, causing water to overflow the land of the plaintiff. Trespass, in one of its nominate forms, would be the proper action. On the other hand, suppose the defendant thoughtlessly permitted the banks of his pond to fall into a state of disrepair, so that the water escaped and overflowed the land of the plaintiff. Trespass, in its nominate forms, would not lie, because the

---

[1] George A. Adams and M. Morse Stephens, *Select Documents of English Constitutional History* (New York: The Macmillan Company, 1901), p. 76.

damage did not result from any intentional act of the defendant, but rather from his inaction. In both cases the land of the plaintiff was inundated, and damage resulted. To the plaintiff, the cases were indistinguishable. To the law they were not comparable.

Cases of damage caused by inactivity, or nonfeasance, came to be cognizable under the innominate action of trespass on the case. In the course of time, some of these actions became so common that they acquired names, such as the action on the case in assumpsit which, ultimately, gave rise to our modern contract action. The law of nuisance, derived from an ancient action, grew into the action on the case for nuisance. Another was deceit, which gave the plaintiff damages for loss of property occasioned by another's misrepresentation.

Negligence

It is impossible to trace the development of the modern law of negligence out of the old law of trespass. Analogies, precursors, and foreshadowings appear throughout the centuries, but in the nineteenth century the doctrine of negligence emerged fully from its cocoon, and its predecessors gradually disappeared.

To some extent, the history of negligence is intertwined with the development of the innominate action of trespass on the case. In that action, the idea of liability from inaction or from indirect injury found early recognition.

Another thread of source material was the duty of care imposed by law upon certain persons by reason of their callings. The common callings, those of veterinarian, surgeon, and ferryman, for instance, were responsible to their customers for damage caused by their inaction. In other words, they were responsible for not performing carefully the duties they claimed they could perform.

In one of the earliest cases involving this type of duty, the *Humber Ferry Case* decided in 1348, a ferryman overloaded his boat with horses, and the plaintiff's horse slipped overboard and was drowned. There was no willful act on the part of the defendant, yet it appears that the action of trespass, not case, was appropriate.[2] The basis of liability was that by virtue of taking his calling, the defendant had imposed upon himself the duty of competence with respect to his customers. The breach of this duty resulted in liability. This bears a resemblance to the modern idea of negligence.

Down to the nineteenth century, the law did not recognize negligence as we understand it. Its main distinction was between direct injury and consequential injury and may be illustrated as follows: Suppose one throws a large rock into a road, not aiming at anything or intending to hit anything. It actually hits A's car. This is direct or immediate injury. Sup-

---

[2] Some authorities, however, consider the action to be an early example of case. See A. K. R. Kiralfy, ed., *Potter's Historical Introduction to English Law and Its Institutions,* 4th ed. (London: Sweet & Maxwell, Ltd., 1958), p. 461 n.

pose, on the other hand, the stone does not hit anything immediately, but that a car comes along later and the driver, not seeing it, runs into the stone, causing injury. This is indirect or consequential injury.

The common law, on this basis, created these distinctions: If an injury was caused by some willful action, the proper remedy would lie in one of the nominate forms of trespass, if immediate and direct injury had resulted. If, on the other hand, injury was caused by nonfeasance, or inaction, the proper remedy would lie in the innominate forms of trespass. An intermediate area which gave much trouble to the lawyers was that of misfeasance, which is neither willful nor, strictly speaking, nonwillful. It is doing something, but doing it improperly. Here the proper form of action (nominate or innominate) depended upon whether the resulting injury was direct or consequential. If it resulted in direct injury, the nominate trespass writs would lie; if it was consequential, the writ of trespass on the case would lie. The liability of those in the common callings, for instance, was for misfeasance (not performing assumed duties skillfully, although without any allegation of willfully producing the injury), and would lie in the nominate trespass writs if the injury done was immediate and direct, rather than consequential.

It is clear, therefore, that our modern distinction between willful and negligent acts cannot be compared with the direct-or-consequential-injury analysis of the common-law forms of action. Lawyers under the writ system were interested in what happened; we are interested in why it happened. The lack of any coherent theory of liability was the root of much confusion in the law of torts until the late nineteenth century.

Modern negligence theory. Early tentative steps toward the modern theory of negligence can be seen in the beginning of the nineteenth century. Arguments pressed by counsel for plaintiffs, sometimes defeated, often contained the germs of a legal idea that later developed into law.

In the 1834 case of *Langridge v. Levy,*[3] counsel for the plaintiff put forward the heroic argument that "wherever a duty is imposed on a person by contract or otherwise, and that duty is violated, anyone who is injured by the violation of it may have a remedy against the wrongdoer. . . ." For the excellent judicial reason that it did not know where such a broad path might lead, the court rejected this proposed test of liability and adopted a narrower ground.

An 1883 English case, *Heaven v. Pender,*[4] was finally able to pose a test which could be accepted as valid in the light of past cases. It stated the legal question in this manner: "What is the proper definition of the relation between two persons other than the relation established by contract or fraud, which imposes on the one of them a duty toward the other to observe, with regard to the person or property of such other, such ordinary care or skill as may be necessary to prevent injury to his person or property?" The court answered its own question.

---

[3] 2 Meeson & Welsby 519.
[4] 52 L.T.J.N.S., Q.B. 702.

. . . whenever one person is by circumstances placed in such a position with regard to another that every one of ordinary sense who did think would at once recognize that if he did not use ordinary care and skill in his own conduct with regard to those circumstances, he would cause danger of injury to the person or property of the other, a duty arises to use ordinary care and skill to avoid such danger.

With this case and others that adopted the same general reasoning, the old distinction between direct and consequential injury disappeared. The important distinction became that between willful and negligent acts; and in the case of negligence, the test for liability required, in addition, a duty to be owed to the injured party.

The test proposed in *Heaven v. Pender* answered no questions. But it did open the door to a continually expanding scope of duty and resultant liability. That has been the subsequent history of the law of torts with regard to the action of negligence.

The question of liability is no longer whether a particular case fits within a particular form of action. It is rather the much more sensible one of how far the courts are willing to go to compensate injury caused by another, however unintentionally. Apparently they are not willing to make one responsible for all consequences traceable to his acts, despite the fact that injury may have been caused by those actions. That would lead to a standard of absolute liability which, some students have said, would negate the progress of a thousand years.

Economic forces

The development of tort law is the story of an accommodation to the fact that more people and more machines result in more accidents. Early tort law reflected the violence of its age: beatings, woundings, and assaults—all generally willful. But as society became more sophisticated, so did the law of torts. In the course of less than a century, the law abandoned old theories of liability that could not cope with the new commercial, mechanical, and manufactured dangers of the Industrial Revolution, and it created the theory of negligence—an open-ended doctrine.

The modern tendency clearly is toward an ever-increasing area of liability in negligence. This gives satisfaction to plaintiffs who, naturally, feel that injury should be compensated by the party who caused it, whether it was willful, negligent, or not. Courts are shifting the risk of activity increasingly from the injured party to the one whose action or inaction caused the injury. And adequately financed insurance is shifting the risk of activity to the public at large. Through premium payments we all bear the financial burdens of one another's activities. Insured drivers, for instance, pay proportionately for the negligent driving of all.

Contracts

10

"CONTRACT" IS A WORD OF LEGAL ART. IT involves the enforceability of a promise or of mutual promises executory in nature, that is, to be carried out in the future. Contract law concerns the elements that make such promises enforceable by the courts.

In viewing the history of contracts in Anglo-American law, two things must constantly be kept in mind. First, we must distinguish the formal from the informal contract. A formal contract is a written document, classically under seal; an informal contract may be either implied from the facts of a situation or expressed in speech or writing. Second, it is necessary to remember that formal and informal contracts are derived from different sources. The common, or informal, contract grew out of the writ of trespass on the case, by a tortuous route. The formal contract is much older and was born in a day that gave legal significance to solemn acts, particularly when accompanied by some ceremonial element.

Early forms in the nature of contract

It was not in the nature of early royal law to enforce mutual promises. This did not mean, however, that such promises could be breached indiscriminately. The church courts, partly on the basis of Roman law and partly on the basis of theology, undertook to recognize promises solemnly entered into, on the theory that the breach of a serious promise involved a breach of faith—a moral matter over which the church claimed jurisdiction. In these courts, therefore, a promise, if accompanied by so little as a handclasp, was recognized as binding.

It appears that in the communal and seignorial courts also, remedies were given to recipients of broken promises. Cases that survive from those courts indicate that damages ·or distraint could be imposed against one who did not perform the equivalent of a modern contractual obligation.

The common-law courts, however, did not extend remedies to these promises, whether the type enforced in the local courts or the *fides facta* of the church courts, where there was breach of a promise in which one had "made his faith" by some solemn act such as a handclasp. In fact, to limit the jurisdiction of the church courts to spiritual matters, royal courts from time to time issued prohibitions demanding that church courts desist from enforcing such promises.

The early royal courts came closest to enforcing contracts through the concept of a pledge. If a person made a promise and posted a pledge to guarantee performance, the promisee might forfeit the pledge upon failure to perform. This, however, bears only a vague resemblance to enforcement of the promise itself.

Common-law actions in the nature of contract. Some common-law writs bear a resemblance to modern contract and, to be sure, were predecessors of contract law, supplying some of its present elements.

DEBT. The earliest writ was the action of debt, probably adopted from prior practice in the local courts. In the time of Glanvill (*c.* 1187) an early and expensive form of the writ was mentioned; in the next fifty years it developed into a rather definite form and was appropriate in the following cases:

For the recovery of money loaned. The theory was not that the defendant was liable on his promise to repay, but that he must pay for the benefit received.

For the agreed price of goods sold and delivered. This was also based on the benefit received by the defendant and did not, in theory, depend on any promise to pay. The plaintiff had to show his *quid pro quo,* the benefit of the goods received by the defendant.

For rent due under a lease.

For money which a court had determined was due to a party.

For money due from a surety.

In the early period, for failure to perform a promise, in writing and under seal, to pay a fixed sum of money.

More will be said of the seal in connection with the action of covenant.

COVENANT. The action of covenant was devised about the year 1200 for the restricted purpose of protecting lessees against breaches of duty by their lessors. The possessory assizes protected only freehold estates, and a lease was not a freehold. From this limited use, covenant spread to the creation of family settlements, whereby one conveyed land to another with the understanding that he would reconvey in accordance with the settlement. To obtain a legal and binding obligation from this intermediate party, a formal writing called a covenant was resorted to.

By 1284 (the Statute of Wales) it was clear that covenants could be used to bind one to any promise except a debt (and there already was an action for that). Covenant was the common law's closest approximation to the concept of a contractual duty.

By the end of the thirteenth century it was required that the writing must have the seal of the promisor affixed to it. The seal previously had been used in the action of debt to prove the validity of the document. If it was sealed, it was genuine, but if it was not sealed, the defendant was free to prove it fraudulent.

In the absence of a seal, the method of proof was wager of law. This ancient device permitted a defendant to support his denial by bringing a number of oathhelpers who swore that the defendant was a truthful man but did not swear to the truth of this particular denial. In the action of covenant, the seal was transmuted from an evidentiary proof of validity to a requisite: without the seal, there was no covenant.

Actions on sealed instruments continue, in some American jurisdictions, to this day. In such cases the contract, called a formal contract, is enforced without regard to the existence of consideration or to the techniques of offer and acceptance. Although it is based on ancient practice, in some cases the sealed instrument performs a useful function. If, for instance, one wishes to bind himself legally to a promise to make a future gift in such a jurisdiction, he need only write: "I promise to pay John Doe $500 on June 1, 1964. (sgd) Richard Roe (seal)"

DETINUE. The third action, detinue, probably was an offshoot of the action of debt. If an article was kept (detained) after its owner demanded it, even without prior agreement to return the chattel, the writ of detinue could be used for recovery or for obtaining money damages.

Originally, detinue was based on a bailment (the delivery of temporary possession of goods) and refusal to return. If A, for instance, loaned a plow to B, to be returned at the end of a week, A had an action in detinue against B if B failed to return the plow as agreed. Subsequently, however, detinue would lie for recovery of a chattel even where there was no bailment, and so lost any contractual element it may have contained. Still later it was adapted to recovery of the price due on a contract of sale; but this occurred after the development of modern contract law and may be explained on that basis.

ACCOUNT. The last of these precontract actions was that of account. Probably developed in the early thirteenth century, it was available against a defendant who had received property from the plaintiff for the benefit of the plaintiff. In that way it can be distinguished from detinue, where the bailment was for the benefit of the defendant. Account was originally the remedy of a landowner against bailiffs who had received money or goods on his behalf. From that point it was extended to lie against agents, partners, and those who held funds for investment. It did not give a remedy, however, against those entrusted with land. To the extent that it required the defendant to return something he previously had promised to return, account had in it some elements of contract. Basically, however, it was founded on the theory of the existence of a formal relationship—bailiff, agent, or partner—which gave rise to a duty to account. A breach of duty, not of promise, gave rise to the action.

Fate of these actions. Debt, covenant, detinue, and account foreshadow contract but were not based on any theory of enforceable promises. For reasons individual to each, they were destined to be replaced or superseded. In debt and detinue, wager of law was a valid defense, and as time went on, that defense became more and more undesirable in the thinking of parties plaintiff. Debt was superseded by the modern contract action, and detinue by a newer and more extensive action called trover. Covenant became confined to actions on sealed documents, and thus its scope was severely circumscribed. It has, however, survived in some jurisdictions. Account was hemmed in with procedural defects that made it time-consuming and that, together with other defects, caused it to be superseded by another procedure of the same name developed in the Court of Chancery.

Trespass on the case on an assumpsit

Although the concepts of trespass and contract appear to be separated by a wide conceptual gulf, they spring from a common source. The word connecting the two concepts is "duty." A basic ingredient of the law of torts is the existence and breach of a duty, and the assumption of a duty is part of every contract. In tort law, duties are socially imposed; but in the case of a contract, the duty is voluntarily assumed by agreement.

An early type of enforceable duty which illustrates this connection is the duty of a person following a common calling (a veterinarian, ferryman, or smith). These people had imposed on them by law the duty to act in accordance with the usual standards of their callings. If they failed to do so, an injured customer could bring an action of trespass against them.

Two things should be noticed about the position of the common callings. First, the duty was considered to be socially imposed and not voluntarily assumed. Second, injured persons were harmed in their persons or property because something was done improperly (a malfeasance) and not because nothing was done (a nonfeasance).

Today we might conceive the duty of a veterinarian, for instance, to be a contractual duty, because the veterinarian makes a contract properly to treat the animal of his customer. At the time of which we are speaking, however, contract had not come into being, and the duty of the veterinarian was socially imposed: his breach of duty by careless treatment was a tort. There was no remedy, as there might be today, merely for not treating the animal.

Attempts to include actions for a pure nonfeasance under the forms of trespass were made in the early fifteenth century, but were not upheld by the courts. A mere nonfeasance was not a trespass. A tort remedy would lie only for doing something, but doing it improperly, and not for failing to do it. In the absence of a covenant, the courts were unwilling to hold one to a promise, but they agreed that if the promised act had been attempted and had been done badly, relief might be granted.

Another area of law, however, converged on this development and led to an accommodation. The ancient action of deceit, which dates back to the early thirteenth century, had come, by the fifteenth century, to include actions which we might denominate breach of warranty. If a person accompanied a sale of goods with an express warranty, a breach of that warranty could be remedied in the courts by an action of trespass on the case for deceit. To modern law this would be an action in contract, for the promise (in the form of a warranty) is what is being sued on. To medieval law, however, it was an action based on deceit.

The action of deceit.   Cases make law; but since the facts of future cases are beyond the control of the courts, the law often is fashioned by accident. *Somerton's Case* is an instance.[1] In that case, a lawyer was to see the conveyance of land to his client; but contrary to his undertaking, he had it conveyed to another person. This was not a true case of nonfeasance, however; for in addition to the fact that the lawyer did not perform his undertaking for his client (his assumpsit), he did something wrong: he had the property conveyed to another person. The argument for deceit made in *Somerton's Case* came to fruition in *Doige's Case,*[2] nine years later. There we see treated as a deceit the defendant's sale to a third party, in contravention of an undertaking already paid for, to convey to the plaintiff. The fact that the plaintiff might have had an action for breach of covenant was immaterial.

These cases have been extensively analyzed, and it has been maintained that some of the judges believed that mutual executory promises could be enforced in favor of a buyer who had agreed to pay a set price. This contention was supported by an analogy to the action of debt, which by that time permitted the seller to sue the buyer if the buyer had agreed to pay a fixed price for certain goods and had refused to accept them.

It is true that debt had come to include such an action by the seller. That result had occurred, however, because there had been a coterminous movement in the law to recognize the passage of title (property) in personal property at the moment an agreement was made to pay a fixed price for specific goods (a sum certain) although delivery was to be postponed. At the moment of the agreement, the buyer obtained title but not possession. Therefore if the seller refused to deliver the goods, the buyer, being entitled to the exact goods, could bring an action of detinue. A second point to the argument is this: if the goods belong to the buyer, although not yet delivered, it follows that the seller has an action of debt against the buyer if the buyer refuses to take the goods. This latter argument, however, scarcely could apply to a conveyance of land, because the common law, in theory, still required livery of seisin to constitute an effective enfeoffment. Title to the land could not pass before "delivery."

---

[1] 1433. See William S. Holdsworth, *A History of English Law,* 5th ed. (London: Methuen & Co., Ltd., 1942), III, 431-34.
[2] 1442. *Ibid.,* pp. 435-39.

Since the buyer had no right to, or action for, the land, the seller could not sue for the price. He had not surrendered either title or seisin. The attempted analogy, although ingenious, was inapt.

Through the remainder of the fifteenth century the basis for relief still was something more than a mere nonfeasance—in addition to not selling the land to the prospective and agreed buyer, the seller had to make it impossible to do so by selling it to another.

In the early sixteenth century, however, there occurred a further advance which gave a remedy for the failure to sell even though the property had not been sold to another—a pure case of nonfeasance. In such a case, however, the plaintiff had suffered a loss because he already had paid the purchase price. This also was true of later cases in which defendants were held liable for failure to pay for goods delivered at their request to other persons.

The action of deceit, at the beginning of the sixteenth century, was still concerned with something more than mere naked promises, for in all cases the plaintiff had performed his share of the bargain, at least in part, by payment of some or all of the purchase price. It was to be some time before the common-law courts granted relief when the plaintiff had not sustained some loss, even though the defendant had not been enriched.

Since some loss to the plaintiff by way of payment or delivery of goods was necessary to these cases, they fit with trespass theory, which is based on injury. Modern contract, to be sure, requires loss, but in a different sense. Contract loss is in point of conjecture, and not necessarily out-of-pocket. Contract loss, for instance, can be the difference between the contract price and the market price of goods sold, which is pure expectation. The loss in these cases was not an expectation loss, but an out-of-pocket loss.

Up to this point, then, the following picture emerges. First, if a person started to perform according to the terms of an undertaking (either as implied by law or as agreed by the parties) and did it badly (a malfeasance), he was liable in the action of trespass. Second, if a person agreed to perform and accepted the other party's money (thus deriving a benefit) but failed to perform at all (a nonfeasance) he was liable in an action based on a deceit. Trespass came to include the performance of requested acts which did not benefit the promisor. If, for instance, A had said to B, "Supply C with a shirt," and B had done so, the action of case would have lain against A for failing to pay as promised, although A did not get the shirt. B, however, had been deprived of it.

Mutual executory promises. The next step was the giant one, to the modern doctrine of the enforceability of mutual executory promises regardless of whether a direct loss was incurred by the plaintiff. This was accomplished through the King's Bench writ commonly called indebitatus assumpsit.

Basically, indebitatus assumpsit was one of the allegations (or counts) within the action of trespass on the case on an assumpsit. The plaintiff might have alleged a sale of goods out of which a duty to pay arose, and a subsequent promise to pay. To be sure, an action of debt could be brought in Common Pleas on the original bargain and sale if the price was certain, without regard to the subsequent promise to pay; however, this later promise and its breach were the bases for the count of indebitatus assumpsit. The words of the count are significant because they mean, literally, "being indebted, he assumed." This form of action appeared in the middle of the sixteenth century as an alternative to the action of debt.

King's Bench, in a further attempt to obtain concurrent jurisdiction with Common Pleas, extended this action by the fiction that if a debt existed, a subsequent promise to pay would be assumed, even though not expressly made. Indebitatus assumpsit, the King's Bench action, would lie, therefore, as an exact alternative to the Common Pleas action of debt. This, presumably, was to the liking of plaintiffs because of the cheaper and quicker processes of King's Bench and because of the availability of trial by jury (instead of wager of law, which attended the action of debt).

In 1602 the celebrated litigation in *Slade's Case* [3] arose. The facts were simple. Slade alleged that he had bargained and sold certain wheat and rye growing on his land to Morley, who promised to pay. On breach, he sued Morley in indebitatus assumpsit. The jury found, by special verdict, "that the defendant bought the wheat and rye from the plaintiff . . . and that there was no other promise or assumption between the plaintiff and the defendant except the said bargain. . . ." [4] This, of course, posed the crucial question. The action of debt clearly could have been brought on the original sale of the rye and wheat. The action of indebitatus assumpsit could have been brought had a subsequent promise been made. The jury found, however, that no such later promise had been made.

The defendant strenuously objected to the action on the ground that he could not wage his law in indebitatus assumpsit, but could have done so had the action of debt been brought. The case reports the defendant's claim "that the maintenance of this action takes away the defendant's benefit of wager of law, and thus bereaves him of the benefit that the law gives him, which is his birthright; perhaps the defendant has paid or satisfied the plaintiff in private between themselves alone, of which payment or satisfaction he has no one to testify, and therefore it would be mischievous if he could not wage his law in such case. . . ." [5]

The trial was adjourned, and the point was argued in numerous conferences before all the justices of England and barons of the exchequer. It was decided, ultimately, that the action was correct. The opinion ended with the words which became the foundation of modern contract law:

> It was resolved, that every contract executory imports in itself an assumpsit, for when one agrees to pay money, or to deliver anything, he thereby assumes or promises to pay or deliver it, and thus when one sells any goods to another, and agrees to deliver them at a future day, and the other in consideration thereof agrees to pay such a sum at such a day, in that case both parties may have their actions of debt, or actions

[3] 4 Rep. 92b.
[4] *Ibid.*
[5] *Id.* at 92b-93a.

on the case on an assumpsit, for the mutual executory agreement of both parties imports in itself reciprocal actions upon the case, in addition to actions of debt. . . .[6]

Assumpsit, therefore, which started as a mere supplement to the action of debt, effectively displaced it as a result of this decision.

Contracts implied in fact and quasi contracts

Slade's Case, although momentous from the point of view of future developments, decided a relatively minor point at the time: that a bargain in which the price was agreed was in itself, without a subsequent promise, a sufficient basis for an action of assumpsit. There still remained, however, the problem of the unpaid seller who had delivered goods to another without an express agreement on the price. In such a case, the action of debt would not lie, for there was no sum certain (agreed and specific price) involved. The action of assumpsit would not lie, for no express promise to pay had been made. A remedy for this situation had to await the early seventeenth century, when the law saw fit to imply a promise to pay a reasonable price when the buyer, at his request, had received goods or services.

This development gave rise to the modern implied contract (contract implied in fact). The seller can recover the reasonable price of his merchandise (*quantum valebat*), and the one who renders services can recover their reasonable value (*quantum meruit*), although there has been no agreement on a specific price.

There were, in addition, cases in which an implied promise to pay was difficult to find, but there was little doubt that the defendant had been unjustly enriched. These started with cases imposing liability for money due because of some statute. In such a case no promise of the defendant was involved, but merely a statutory liability. Such a case merely resembles contractual liability and is therefore called quasi contract, or contract implied in law. This was extended to the recovery of money received by a person not entitled to it for a variety of reasons, such as double payment of one debt.

The doctrine of consideration

The development of modern contract forced the law, eventually, to determine a means for separating enforceable contracts from agreements that the law considers not sufficiently important to warrant legal enforcement. Early English law attempted to solve the problem by requiring some formality—a handclasp, the handing over of a wand or a piece of wood, the payment of earnest money, and the seal.

In the action of indebitatus assumpsit it was general practice from the early sixteenth century to insert the words "in consideration of" before a

---

[6] *Id.* at 94a-94b.

recital of the prior indebtedness that formed the basis of the action. The clause stated that the subsequent promise had been given "in consideration of" the prior indebtedness. When the subsequent promise became unnecessary, the consideration clause became meaningless. But the idea remained that the defendant made the promise because he had received something.

In the action of debt, it was essential that there be a *quid pro quo* (a "this for that"), the benefit the recipient of the article had received; for instance, the article delivered. In the action of assumpsit, basically a trespass action, the concept of injury or detriment was present. The plaintiff had suffered an injury or detriment by the deceit, for instance, of the defendant; therefore, the defendant should pay.

These two ideas, of benefit to the person making the promise and detriment to the person to whom the promise was given, are the twin bases of our modern doctrine of consideration. Conceived as simply as possible, consideration is the price one pays for the promise of another. In present-day thinking, one must, in return for another's promise, either forbear or promise to forbear from an act he has a legal right to do, or perform or promise to perform an act he is under no legal duty to do. Normally these acts or promises are of benefit to the promisor. In any event, they are a legal detriment to the recipient of the promise—the promisee.

It appears that until the seventeenth century, there was no formal dogma concerning consideration. Earlier, the courts enforced bargains based on moral consideration or obligation, in the manner of Continental and canon law. During the seventeenth century, however, the ideas of benefit and detriment, derived respectively from the actions of debt and assumpsit, bore fruit.

Ultimately, it became clear that benefit alone was an uncertain basis on which to fashion the distinction between enforceable and unenforceable promises. Consequently, the modern law tends to look to some detriment or deprivation of a legal right on the part of the promisee. Courts enforce promises because the recipient of the promise, in return for the promise and as its agreed price, agrees to surrender some part of his legal liberty to do as he pleases. The idea of injury, derived from trespass law, has dominated and has virtually overcome the concept of a benefit received, which was part of the law of debt.

Economic forces

In this survey of the development of contract law we have traversed a period extending from the beginnings of the English common law to the seventeenth century. The need for contracts is a need of a commercial, not an agricultural, society. When commerce was of relatively little importance, when the manorial system was the productive pivot of society, there was little need for enforcement of mutual executory promises. The ancient actions of debt and covenant, and the law of merchants enforced in periodic fairs, in the staple cities, and to some extent in the borough courts, were quite sufficient to meet the economic needs of society.

The press of cases which provided the occasion for the development of a theory of contract law began, as has been noticed, in the fifteenth century, became considerably stronger in the sixteenth century, and resulted in a virtually complete legal response in the seventeenth and eighteenth centuries. This evolution coincides almost exactly with the breakdown of the manorial system in England and the development of a mercantilist, and subsequently capitalist, economic system.

Although the manors had been virtually self-sufficient economic entities until the thirteenth century, that period saw the timorous beginnings of the enclosure movement, a tendency of landlords to make their own sheepwalks from common land previously available for pasturage. Trade was increasing, and wool was a profitable item of commerce. The enclosure movement was followed in the succeeding centuries by the abandonment of the traditional organization of agriculture. Tenants were forced off the land into the growing cities, in order that a more advanced organization of agriculture might take the place of the ancient manor—all this occurred in search of the money needed to satisfy the increasing demands of the propertied classes.

This in turn created a reservoir of labor pressing for employment in the cities and towns, employed by a new class of manufacturers whose competition with the older guildsmen resulted, ultimately, in the creation of a new economic order. Feudalism, which had started as a military system and then had changed into a social system based on the ownership of land, was destroyed by extensive trade and manufacturing, new modes of producing wealth. For these the development of contract law was essential.

The law of contracts, therefore, was a response to economic change. It was not created through any planned growth. On the contrary, the growth of the law was limited and directed by its need to remain in touch with the past. The only way the law could grow was through expansion of the ancient forms of action, in this case the action of trespass. It is notable that nowhere in this evolution, except for the Statute of Frauds (1677), does a statute appear. Almost involuntarily, and perhaps unwittingly, the common-law judges (with some prodding from their colleagues in the Chancery) developed doctrines which responded to social needs, and they did it through the slow evolution of judge-made case law.

❧ PART IV

The
Common Law
Codified

The law and commerce –
action and reaction

11

ALTHOUGH THE COMMON LAW HAS AL-
ways responded to the pressures of society, in no area
is the effect of that pressure quite so clear as in commercial law. Commercial law includes the law concerning transfer of rights in personal property (the
law of sales) and intangible rights to sue (the law of
assignments and commercial paper), the law of business organizations (partnerships and corporations),
of business representation (agency), of shipping, and
of insurance.

Trade can exist only when society reaches a stage
in which some areas have surplus production and
other areas are in need of that surplus and have something to offer in exchange. Then there must be a means
to transport goods from one place to another and persons willing to engage in that endeavor. So long as a
given society is basically agricultural and self-sufficient, trade finds an insignificant place. When a
society starts to become urbanized, however, the stage
for commerce is set, for rarely can all the needs and
wants of the citizens be met locally.

From that point, the development of trade depends
upon conditions favorable to traders: roads and ships,
a medium of exchange, a system of commercial rules
or laws. There must be standard weights and measures, a system of credit, and devices for accumulation
of capital. Agents become necessary for representation, and everyone must work in an ethical climate
that favors trade and provides some political stability.

Early mercantile law

These conditions have existed at many times and in many places in the Western world. Ancient Greece was acquainted with trade, but its basic political instability and unwillingness to develop foreign markets as sources of supply restrained commercial development. Rome developed trade to a much greater extent, but the position and prestige of traders was never sufficiently high to give them influence in the formation of the law. Such influence is essential if more than the rudimentary needs of trade are to be met by a legal system; for if groups inimical to traders formulate the law, it is highly unlikely that the law will reflect the needs of trade.

This theory can be supported by examples of communities with favorable legal climates. Rhodes, a community largely dependent upon trade, created a basic law of the sea during the third and second centuries B.C., which many subsequent codes followed, and ". . . all sea-law for the ensuing thousand years was known as the Rhodian law." [1] After the conquest and decline of Rome, merchants in Italy and southern Europe often obtained control of the governments of cities, and each of these towns created its own basic laws of commerce. Amalfi, near Naples, had such a code in the eleventh century, and Barcelona in the twelfth. Oleron, an island (then owned by England) in the Bay of Biscay, also had such a code in the twelfth century. The codes of the Mediterranean area were compiled in the fifteenth century into a collection known as the *Consolato del Mare*, which became dominant in that area.

A different approach was followed in the north of Europe. Rather than through overt control, as in the southern cities, the power of merchants was expressed through franchises obtained from government, which entitled merchants to create their own rules of law and to enforce these rules through their own courts. Franchises to hold fairs were temporary; but the franchises of the staple cities, empowered to deal in certain basic commodities, were permanent. Because Italian law had developed earlier than the law in northern Europe, the northerners modeled their own law after it. Consequently there arose the laws of Wisby, and those of the Hanseatic League (which was in existence from the fourteenth to the seventeenth centuries). By the beginning of the modern period of trade expansion, the dominant codes were those of Oleron, Wisby, the Hanseatic League, and the *Consolato del Mare*.

Although Roman law provided a theoretical model for the development of these codes and although many of its concepts were adopted and followed, in specific details the Roman law concerning trade was not so highly developed as the city codes of the seventeenth century. In fact, the attempted revival of Roman law in Italy during that time tended to postpone the development of modern rules in some areas of law.[2]

---

[1] John Henry Wigmore, *A Panorama of the World's Legal Systems* (Washington: Washington Book Company, 1936), p. 880.
[2] Holdsworth, *History of English Law*, VIII, 142.

English commercial law followed northern European practices, basically the laws of Oleron. Commercial law based on these universal principles was used in the franchised courts of the fairs and in the separate courts of the boroughs. Many trading towns had their own adaptations of commercial law, such as the Oak Book of Southampton, the Red Book of Bristol, and, with the creation of an Admiralty jurisdiction, the Black Book of the Admiralty.

The seventeenth century movement toward national governments resulted in a decline of separate mercantile franchises and their courts. The staple towns, for instance, had outlived their usefulness. When the law merchant became incorporated into a national system of laws enforced by national courts of general jurisdiction, the local codes were finally extinguished. But national systems of law necessarily depended upon the older codes for their stock of ideas and on the changing customs of merchants for new developments.

The development of trade

From the fall of Rome until the eleventh century, there was little trade in Europe. The first post-Roman revival of trade came about in the eighth century through the efforts of the Arabs, followed by the Lombards, who were the first European trading group to bring commerce to all of Europe, including England. The Crusades introduced Europeans to the exotic products of the East, and the resulting demand created a further stimulated trade.

English trade was dominated by aliens until the late fourteenth century. The manorial system, virtually self-sufficient, started to break down after the Black Death (1348-1349), and the subsequent growth of towns with a surplus of labor led in turn to the dissolution of the restrictive guild system and the growth of an indigenous merchant class with demands of its own. Ultimate political representation of the middle class in the House of Commons and the passage of legislation to spur commerce created a favorable climate for mercantile development. Commercial practices were significant in creating the common law, a fact that was recognized by important judges who led the way to complete integration of the two.

Commercial law is the story of the confrontation of the common-law courts and the trading community. England was ceasing to be an agricultural community and was emerging as the dominant trading center of the world. The common law could not permit commercial law to continue to develop along independent lines, and it yet was unable fully to conform to business needs. How an accommodation was accomplished in the areas of negotiable instruments and business organizations must next be considered.

Negotiable instruments

12

THE WIDESPREAD LAWS OF MERCHANTS are commonly referred to as the *lex mercatoria,* or law merchant, and may be divided into two parts: admiralty law, dealing with maritime commerce, and commercial law, dealing with commerce ashore. Space forbids dealing with maritime law; the parts of commercial law here considered are the law of negotiable instruments, partnerships, and corporations.

Types of negotiable instruments

There are two basic negotiable instruments which, although they have totally different purposes, have three indispensable features in common. The first such instrument is the promissory note, an evidence of indebtedness. It indicates that one person, the maker, owes money to the other, the payee. The second type is an order to pay, called a draft, or, earlier, a bill of exchange. One person, the drawer, orders another, the drawee, to pay a certain sum of money to a third person, called the payee. The most common example is the simple bank check.

The three features these instruments share in common are: (1) they are readily transferable (negotiable) from one person to another, (2) the ultimate holder can sue on them in his own name, and (3) the ultimate holder for value and in good faith takes good title to a genuine instrument free of prior defects. Two examples may suffice.

1. A maker signs a promissory note payable to the

order of a payee, in return for the payee's promise to deliver goods in the future. The payee negotiates the note to a holder, who is a good-faith purchaser for value, but then the payee does not deliver the goods to the note's maker. The holder demands payment from the maker, who defends on the ground that the promised goods were not delivered. The maker's defense, although good against the payee, is futile. He must pay the holder.

2. The same result would follow if, instead of giving the payee a note, the purchaser drew a check on the drawee bank to the payee's order, and the check came into the hands of a good-faith holder for value.

It is important to keep in mind that an instrument payable to a named payee only, without mentioning another possible holder (by adding the words "or order" after the name of the payee) has never created a fully negotiable instrument. The three features mentioned do not apply to such a nonnegotiable instrument.

The promissory note and the draft, commonly treated together today, are the result of different although related lines of development; therefore, they will be considered separately.

The bill of exchange, or draft

The bill of exchange, now commonly called a draft, is a basic and essential commercial instrument. When merchants deal with one another, respective debits and credits arise. These can be settled by the transfer of money, but apparently every trading group that ever has developed considerable trade has found it more advantageous and considerably safer to settle accounts by means of some commercial document similar to the draft.

Suppose, for instance, that A, a medieval French merchant, desired to purchase goods from B, a merchant in Italy. A might, conceivably, have sent payment to B in coin or bullion in the custody of a servant. But it would have been much more convenient for A to go to another French merchant, C, who had a credit with another Italian merchant, D, and have C prepare a document ordering his Italian merchant debtor, D, to pay the needed sum to B.

These were the parties to the original bill of exchange: A, the purchaser, B, the payee, C, the drawer, and D, the drawee. Notice that there were four parties to this transaction instead of the three parties to the modern draft.

Early enforcement. This device appeared as early as the fourteenth century in Europe, and it was used in England in the sixteenth and early seventeenth centuries. It developed out of an even earlier procedure involving the use of agents. Since much medieval trade took place at the periodic local fairs, merchants often arranged to settle their accounts there. Their agents would go to the fair armed with documents authorizing the settling of their respective accounts. Since the fairs were used by merchants from numerous places, they became large clearing houses for the debts of European merchants. The fairs were essential to medieval trade, and only after the sixteenth century were they super-seded by more modern marketing devices.

In all parts of Europe until the nationalization of law in the seven-teenth century, these instruments were enforced in special merchants' courts. In England, courts frequented by merchants were of various types: the courts of the fairs, those of the boroughs, of the staple cities, and the Court of Admiralty (which began in the fourteenth century, but the records of which are available only from the middle of the sixteenth century). Courts of the fairs and boroughs dealt with domestic trade, while those of the staple cities mainly governed foreign trade. The posi-tion of Admiralty varied through the years of its existence, until its juris-diction over commercial matters, as distinguished from maritime matters, was taken over by the common-law courts in the middle of the seventeenth century. By that time, fairs were virtually obsolete, and the monopoly of the staple cities over foreign trade was at an end.

The courts of the boroughs and fairs were important in the develop-ment of negotiable instruments until the seventeenth century, when the common-law courts took over this jurisdiction. Fairs usually were held by lords or churches, but sometimes they were held in boroughs. The franchise to hold a fair included the right to hold a court there. These courts were referred to as the Piepowder courts, probably derived from *pieds poudres,* or the dusty feet of the merchants. Their temporary nature necessitated speedy justice. All sorts of offenses were tried in them, in-cluding forestalling (attempting to raise prices by artifice), use of false measures, theft, assault and battery, interfering with a sale, defamation of credit, breach of express warranty, failure to deliver in accordance with samples, and the like. One interesting feature of these fairs was that a good-faith purchaser of goods in such an open market (called a market overt) obtained good title to the goods, despite the fact that they might have been stolen previously.

Borough courts were concerned with domestic trade of a continuing nature; and since boroughs were also the centers of guilds, they were in-volved with problems concerning apprentices and the liability of mer-chants for contracts of their agents. If foreign merchants were the liti-gants, a jury of foreign merchants was used; if one party was English and the other alien, the membership of the jury reflected an equal di-vision of origin. Market law was a small although significant part of borough law.

By the fifteenth century, English foreign trade was coming into the hands of English merchants who, quite naturally, adopted the Continental bill of exchange developed mainly by the Italians. It appears from a few fragmentary records that these documents were recognized in the Court of Admiralty and the Mayor's Court of London, but there were no cases in the common-law courts until 1602.[1] By that time it was fairly well estab-lished on the Continent that bills of exchange were enforceable and transferable by endorsement.

---

[1] Martin v. Boure (1602). See J. M. Holden, *The History of Negotiable Instruments in English Law* (London: The Athlone Press, 1955), p. 31.

In common-law courts. The common-law courts had great difficulty handling these instruments. Their forms of action were not well suited to them—they had to work through the action of assumpsit in order to give relief. The purchaser of a four-party bill of exchange theoretically could easily sue the drawee if he did not pay the bill, on the theory of injury by reason of the drawee's failure to live up to his undertaking. Problems arose, however, when the payee desired to sue a drawee who had breached his promise to pay the bill of exchange, because the payee had given the drawee no consideration for his promise to honor the bill. (The consideration moved from the purchaser of the bill.) In order to get around that difficulty, it was alleged that the payee was the agent of the purchaser of the bill of exchange when the purchaser obtained the bill from the drawer, originally. Thus, for the purpose of finding consideration, the purchaser and the payee were one party. The purchaser purportedly paid for the bill of exchange on behalf of the payee. This, of course, was total fiction.

Introduction of law merchant to the common law. Such tortuous maneuvers obviously could not long continue if the law was to develop, and the common-law courts therefore turned to the device of permitting the writ of assumpsit to be issued in accordance with the custom of merchants. This required that the alleged mercantile custom be set forth in detail in the pleadings, and then that its existence be proved at the trial. By 1666 it was declared that the law of merchants was part of the common law of England, and therefore need not be specially alleged.[2] It came to be the rule that the proof of a custom of merchants adopted in one case would make that custom part of the law, so that it need not be proved in a subsequent case.

By 1651 the modern three-party bill of exchange (drawer, drawee, and payee) was in use, and it could be payable either to the "order of" or to the "assignee of" the payee. A bill of exchange payable to bearer could be created by leaving the name of the payee blank (rather than by the modern usage of making it payable expressly to "bearer"). This adoption of the custom of merchants created an exception, for these mercantile instruments, to the common-law rule that a contract right could not be assigned.

Assignments at common law. Two difficulties lay in the way of permitting the transfer of an obligation from one creditor to his assignee. First, a debt was deemed to be personal. This concept had much merit in a day when a creditor could imprison his debtor for not paying a debt. While a debtor's original creditor might be a tenderhearted man, not given to such harsh treatment, his assignee might be a merciless person who would put the debtor in prison without compunction.

Second, the common law could not see that there was anything to transfer. Goods of all types could be sold and transferred because they were the subject of manual delivery. A right to sue, however, as a mere intangible "chose in action," had no material substance and therefore was deemed incapable of transfer. The paper which reflected the contract was

---

[2] Woodward v. Rowe (1666), 2 Keb. 105, 132.

tangible, to be sure, but it was mere evidence of the right and not the right itself. (If, for instance, a contract is destroyed by accident, the right it evidenced still exists, although it may be more difficult to prove.) This stress on physical form was important to the common law until very recent times.

The custom of transferring negotiable instruments by endorsements was established among merchants, nevertheless, by the seventeenth century. When the law came to the point of recognizing merchant customs, it recognized such transfers by endorsement but still denied a transfer of a contract right in those areas not coming within mercantile custom.

By the middle of the seventeenth century, therefore, a bill of exchange could be transferred from one party to another by endorsement, and the holder could sue on it in his own name. These accomplishments were made possible by common-law adoption of the customs of merchants.

Although two elements of modern negotiability had been settled, the courts still were reluctant in the middle of the seventeenth century to give the transferee a bill of exchange better title to it than was held by his transferor. The instrument might be subject to such defenses, for instance, as failure of consideration, or that it was given in payment of a gambling debt.

The first case freeing a good-faith holder for value from a defense valid against the payee was decided in 1699.[3] There it was held that one who lost a bill of exchange could not retrieve it once it fell into the hands of such a holder. With this decision we have reached the beginning of the modern development of the bill of exchange.

Promissory notes

The ancestor of the modern promissory note is the old "writing obligatory," a type of document earlier than the bill of exchange, although its successor, the promissory note, received recognition in English law at a later date.

The earliest writings obligatory were of two types: (1) formal documents under seal, and (2) an informal variety, not under seal. The formal document was recognized at common law through the action of covenant, but the informal type was not recognized as valid.

By the seventeenth century the sealed writing could, on the Continent, be made payable to one's creditor or to the bearer. In England, however, such a writing was payable only to the creditor or his attorney-in-fact. The creditor, therefore, might transfer the document to another, but that person would have to sue as the creditor's agent and therefore would be subject to all defenses good against the creditor. He could not sue in his own name, and he would not get a better title than his predecessor had. Some of these documents were payable to the creditor or the "producer" of the document, apparently in an attempt to create bearer instruments, but their validity in the hands of such a producer is questionable.

---

[3] Anon. (1699) 1 Salk. 126, 3 Salk. 71, 1 Ld. Raym. 738. See Holden, *op. cit.*, p. 64.

Importance of the goldsmiths' activities. The forerunners of bankers, goldsmiths were largely responsible for increased use of informal writings obligatory, or promissory notes. Insecurity during the Civil War and the period of the Commonwealth and Protectorate (1649-1660) led people to entrust their gold to the goldsmiths rather than keep it in the form of plate or in the Tower of London, as had been the custom of many. The goldsmiths lent this wealth at interest to the government and to merchants and paid interest to their depositors. The deposits were evidenced by promissory notes. Goldsmiths also started to pay their depositors' debts, on request, using the money left with them.

A few cases involving such promissory notes were heard by the common-law courts in the latter half of the seventeenth century, but no clear trend toward negotiability was apparent. In *Clerke v. Martin* (1702),[4] furthermore, a dictum maintained that they were not negotiable. It stated the unfortunate opinion that while a bill of exchange was transferable because of the custom of merchants, a promissory note, whether to order or in the form of a bearer instrument, was not negotiable. This point was confirmed in 1703 in a case [5] involving it directly.

That decision, by Lord Holt, was based on the idea that promissory notes were new inventions of the goldsmiths and should not be permitted to create law for the courts. Lord Holt thought that the goldsmiths might have achieved their object by drawing a bill of exchange to the order of the drawer (as one makes out a check to himself to obtain cash) and therefore that the promissory note was not commercially essential.

The Statute of Anne. These opinions resulted in the first direct legislative interference in the course of negotiable-instruments law. Although the aptness of Lord Holt's decision is the subject of scholarly controversy, it seems clear that the decision was contrary to the needs and legitimate demands of merchants. The Statute of Anne (1704) [6] consequently was enacted to confer negotiability upon promissory notes, so that a transferee could sue the maker, on either order or bearer instruments, in the manner of bills of exchange.

Subsequent common-law developments

Until the time of statutory codifications in the late nineteenth century, the history of negotiable instruments is one of gradual refinements, culminating during the tenure of Lord Mansfield (1705-1793), Chief Justice of the King's Bench from 1756 to 1788. Mansfield was particularly qualified for the task of redefining commercial law because of his background and predispositions. As a Scotsman he was interested in, and learned in, Scottish law, which was based on the civil-law principles so basic to Continental mercantile law. As an individual, he was inclined to seek advice from merchants concerning mercantile practice and to adopt it as the law. In cases in which the law was in

---

[4] 1 Salk. 129.
[5] Buller v. Crips (1703) 6 Mod. 29.
[6] 3 & 4 Anne, c. 8.

doubt, evidence of mercantile custom was admitted, and Mansfield used merchants on his juries.

The basic conflict to be resolved was one between justice and certainty. An approach to absolute justice would have required that mercantile custom be considered in each case, in order that it might reflect alterations in practice. Certainty, at the opposite end, would require the law to consider no custom. Mansfield's compromise was to admit custom into evidence where the law was uncertain; but once a point was settled, to exclude evidence of custom thereafter. The first case decided the law.

His primary contribution was in the refinement and definition of terms and the rights of parties. To the sparse comments of prior cases he added analysis, reason, and logic. Although it had been decided in 1699 that a good-faith holder for value of a bill of exchange had rights superior to one who lost it, Mansfield gave form and logic to the point in *Miller v. Race*,[7] whence the doctrine is often traced. Another such refinement was the famous case of *Price v. Neal*,[8] holding that a drawee cannot regain the money he has paid out on a forged bill of exchange. The liabilities and rights of the parties to negotiable instruments were thus settled by a series of decisions during Mansfield's tenure.

The codification movement

Further refinement of unsettled points took place both in England and in the United States up to about 1875. By that time, the accumulated mass of decisions appeared to cry for simplification. In this country, the problem was complicated by the fact that the different states had developed different answers to some of the same problems.

The French had organized negotiable-instruments law by an ordinance in 1673, perhaps at too early a state of development. This ordinance, expanded, was incorporated into the French Code of Commerce in 1818.

The codification movement in the area of negotiable instruments started in England.[9] In 1878 Sir Mackenzie Chalmers published his *Digest of the Laws of Bills of Exchange,* distinguished from several prior works on the topic in that it was a series of 287 propositions. The form may have derived from Chalmers' acquaintance with prior eighteenth century codes in British India, where simplified statutes were essential because India had no background of case law on which to rely.

In 1881, Chalmers presented to the British Institute of Bankers a paper on the advantages of codifying the law of negotiable instruments. He received a favorable response. Subsequently, Chalmers prepared a bill based on his book, and Parliament passed it as the Bills of Exchange Act of 1882. In America, the National Conference of Commissioners on Uniform State Laws proposed a Negotiable Instruments Law in 1896, based in large measure on the prior English Bills of Exchange Act of 1882, but

---

[7] (1758) 1 Burr. 452.
[8] (1762) 3 Burr. 1354.
[9] See Chapter 6 for general comments on codification.

reflecting American commercial practice as it differed from the English. This act was the earliest complete success of the National Conference, and all states had adopted it by 1924.

The basic dilemma between justice and certainty was not resolved by this enactment. During the course of the twentieth century two developments took place: (1) the continued change in mercantile practice, and (2) divergent interpretations of particular points by various states. By the 1940's, therefore, it was apparent that the law was out of step with the times and that the divergent interpretations had to be brought together. In addition, it was felt that separate statutes on various areas of commercial law might profitably be combined in one large statute.

The American Law Institute and the National Conference of Commissioners on Uniform State Laws started, in 1945, to create a Uniform Commercial Code covering eight previously separate areas of commercial law, including negotiable paper. Its first official draft was published in 1952 and covered the subject matter of the Negotiable Instruments Law (1896), the Uniform Warehouse Receipts Act (1906), the Uniform Sales Act (1906), the Uniform Bills of Lading Act (1909), the Uniform Stock Transfer Act (1909), the Uniform Conditional Sales Act (1918), and the Uniform Trust Receipts Act (1933).

Subsequent drafts appeared in 1957 and 1958, based on changes suggested by myriad critics, and by 1963 the code was law, or shortly to become effective, in one-quarter of the states.

There is no reason to believe, of course, that this code will solve the basic conflict between justice and certainty. Surely commercial practices will change, and just as surely the law must change in order to reflect market conditions and facilitate commercial activity. To some extent the code incorporates a built-in factor to allow for change by stating, in various places, that the courts shall consider commercial standards in coming to decisions. Such terms as "good faith," "reasonableness," "honesty in fact," "observance of reasonable commercial standards," and "commercial reasonableness" are used to set standards in particular areas. These standards are, generally, the objective standards of the market place and not the subjective standards of a person's individual and private intention. One incisive comment on the code maintains that, in using such terms, it recognizes "as the legal norm for determining controversies the variant rules of conduct observed in actual transaction of business." [10] To some extent, then, commercial change can be automatically incorporated into the law as commercial practices change the nature or content of particular commercial standards.

This, therefore, is the eternal task of commercial law: to determine the approaches and rules that govern commercial transactions; to reflect commercial practice where its effect is beneficial or at least benign, in order to achieve the goal of a legal climate in which commerce can flourish; but not to ignore its duty to strike down practices that are inimical to the public interest.

---

[10] *Report of the Law Review Commission for 1956* (N.Y. State, 1956).

Business organizations

13

THE MODERN BUSINESS CORPORATION IS the legal response to the economic need for a means to amass the tremendous capital needed in modern business. It is a composite of three elements—the concepts of the corporate entity, joint stock, and limited liability—each of which stems from a different source.

The concept of entity is that of the corporation as a legal individual. It may sue and be sued in its own name, own and transfer property, enter into contracts, commit torts and crimes, and do all other things that its nonmaterial nature permits. Since the corporation is an entity, it may be established to exist perpetually.

Joint stock enables the shareholders to transfer their shares during their lives or at death. It is this concept that makes the ownership of a corporation divisible into small shares and, therefore, enables it to draw its capital from a multitude of relatively small investors.

Limited liability protects the shareholder against personal ruin if the corporation fails financially. The shareholders will lose no more than their initial investment commitment or, at most, some excess, fixed by statute, over that investment.

Only the second of these features, joint stock, is essential to the accumulation of large amounts of capital. The theory of entity, although not essential, is desirable, for to require the joinder of all shareholders in suits, contracts, prosecutions, and the other business of a corporation would be unwieldy if not impossible. Even this, however, might have been accomplished under a theory of representation related to that of a trust or an agency. Limited liability, likewise, is not an absolute necessity. If shareholders were merely held immune from personal liability until corporate assets were exhausted, they would have a high degree of immunity from liability in actual practice if not in theory.

Early entity concepts

A corporation is a distinct legal personality apart from its members. As an entity, a corporation has three basic attributes: it can buy, hold, and dispose of property in its own name; it can contract in its own name; and it can sue and be sued in its own name. A corporation need not have limited liability for its owners, or joint stock. These are attributes of business corporations; but charitable, municipal, or governmental corporations do very well without them, because such corporations have no shareholders.

The Roman concept. A legal entity, created by express action of the state, was known to Roman law as a *universitas*. Cities, colonies, brotherhoods of priests, and groups of artisans achieved that status. Some elementary forms of business associations also were given corporate status in certain cases, particularly in ventures such as salt mining, extraction of ores, and collection of taxes.

Churches and universities. Another source of the concept of entity was the medieval Church. Pollock and Maitland consider the theological notion of the Church as the mystical body of Christ an important factor in the development of the corporate idea.[1]

The common law early recognized that property given to the Church no longer belonged to the patron who donated it. Where control lay within the Church, however, was long a problem. Earliest theory avowed that the property belonged to God or to the patron saint of the parish. The clergyman in charge, therefore, was the rector, or administrator, of the property who did not own the property in his own right, but was accountable to the Church in the person of his successor in office. If, for instance, an abbot or bishop made an improper alienation of land under his control, it could be regained not by the monks (who were legally dead), but by his successor.

But where did the ownership lie in the interval of time between the death of one official and the installation of his successor? For a while, title was said to be held "by the walls of the church" or by the "body or the bride of the Redeemer," [2] but this gave way to the view that the Church itself owned the property as part of the *ecclesia universalis* (church universal, indicating the church as a person). The idea of the *ecclesia universalis* is also related to the status of the early English universities, Oxford and Cambridge, which were treated as entities because of ancient usage. The relationship was not in function but in the Roman

---

[1] Pollock and Maitland, *The History of English Law before the Time of Edward I*, I, 479.
[2] *Ibid.*, p. 483.

concept of the *universitas* as an entity which, being nonmaterial and fictitious, was not subject to corporal punishment in this world or the next.

From all this ecclesiastical theory, the common law had to devise a concept for dealing with the mundane interests of the Church. The courts apparently seized upon the idea of representation: the clergy were in a relationship to their property, their Church, and their flocks which made them a type of father or agent or guardian. In that position the Church was, like a minor, sheltered by the courts and given their protection. The idea was not purely corporate, but it had some elements of corporateness.

Boroughs and towns. Before the fourteenth century, boroughs were corporations by prescription, or ancient usage; and after that time, by charter from the Crown. Boroughs had a number of corporate characteristics, including their power to hold borough courts, to compel members of the borough to buy and sell there and to tax their trade, to govern themselves (within limits), to form merchant guilds, and to own land and perhaps some chattels.

Guilds. There were two types of guilds dealing in business: merchant and craft. Merchant guilds were monopolies of retail trade; craft guilds were associations of craftsmen with powers to regulate their memberships.

MERCHANT GUILDS. When the borough merchants' trade became sufficient to justify their membership, they joined a guild. It was an organization separate from the borough or town government, but its influential members might hold offices in both groups. The guild's by-laws reached beyond its membership, regulating trade within the boroughs, and it could buy commodities outside the borough for local sale and profit.

Merchant guilds were powerful from the thirteenth to the fifteenth century. After this period their power decreased, because trade ceased to be a monopoly of the towns. Their contribution to corporate theory was their regulation of borough commerce and transaction of business for a common profit.

CRAFT GUILDS. The second quarter of the twelfth century marked the appearance of the craft guilds. During the reign of Henry II they were sometimes given charters which made them separate, administratively, from their towns. When Richard I (1189-1199) succeeded Henry, however, craft guilds were once more subordinated to town management.

The purpose of the craft guilds, as distinguished from that of the merchant guilds, was economic, not governmental. Their object was to create a class of workmen competent to serve the public. They supervised apprenticeships in their respective crafts, regulated standards of work, and exercised effective control over their own members.

With the loss of power by the merchant guilds after the fifteenth century and the breakdown of borough control over borough commerce, craft guilds expanded. Masters in crafts became managers of businesses. They left their workbenches and became, in effect, members of a monopoly in their crafts. The economic distinction between working artisans and capital-owning masters was recognized by the "livery company," a term derived from the distinctive dress which only the masters were entitled to wear. Masters, who ran their separate businesses, also controlled trade in their crafts by means of regulations binding on all members of these companies.

Many livery companies were granted incorporation or the equivalent by the king. The practice of incorporating these companies dates back at least to 1407 when Henry IV granted the privilege to the haberdashers. The movement gained momentum with the incorporation of the fishmongers in 1433, the vintners in 1437, the merchant tailors in 1466, and the carpenters in 1477. In the sixteenth century, companies of foreign merchants were incorporated. In each of these companies members traded on their separate accounts, but the group had corporate powers. The organization presaged the modern corporation in that its formation was voluntary, it had a common seal, and it could sue and be sued as a unit.

Commenda and societas. On the Continent, other forms of business organization were also used. The *commenda* resembled a modern limited partnership. It combined capital and management by providing for investment of money in return for a share of the profits. The investors did not manage the business, and they had limited liability; the active partners controlled the business. It was not, however, an entity.

The *societas* had some features of corporateness, such as the ability to enter into a contract in its own name. On the other hand, liability of the members was unlimited; each could act for the group, and they were not complete juristic persons.

Joint stock companies

By the sixteenth century, English overseas trade had sufficiently developed to require large capital structures. The joint stock company was devised to meet this need. The first of these were, properly speaking, regulated companies. They received charters from the Crown for their overseas activities, but the members traded for their own profit, and the company itself did not trade. They resembled the guilds in many ways, including their regulatory powers over members. In addition, they were given governmental powers in overseas areas in which they traded. One of the earliest English companies was the Russia Company, formed in 1555. More permanent was the East India Company, formed in 1600. In its earlier form, separate investments were made for each voyage, but in 1613, stock began to be subscribed for a period of years; and in 1657, permanent joint stock was offered. With these changes, the right to trade on the members' private accounts disappeared. When transferability of shares was added to corporate trading, the joint stock company of eighteenth century England was complete.

About the same time, chartered monopolies in trade were extended to companies in England itself. The Mines Royal obtained its charter in 1568; so did the Mineral and Battery Works. During the seventeenth century, charters were granted to the Governor and Company of Copper Mines in England, the Fishery Company, the Company of White Papermakers in England, the Royal Lutestring Company, and others. These companies, distinguished from those trading overseas, had no governmental powers. Their monopolies, moreover, were protected only against competition by other corporations. Individuals could compete with them.

Joint stock companies were of various types. Those dealing overseas uniformly acted under royal charters. Domestic joint stock companies often were voluntary associations formed by contract without charters. The charter was needed in order to achieve perpetuity and, presumably, limited liability. Some charters, nevertheless, did not grant perpetual existence, and limited liability (as will be explained) did not mean what it does today. Without incorporation, vexing problems could arise in suing or being sued, for companies would be treated as if they were partnerships in which all members must be joined. Some of the early American colonies were formed as chartered joint stock companies.

Limited liability

Today, limited liability means that shareholders are not responsible for the debts of the corporation beyond the amount of their subscriptions. Often this is considered a consequence of the theory of entity. That theory, however, supports only the proposition that the debts of the corporation are separate from the debts of its shareholders. The separateness of corporate obligations was observed as early as 1441 in England,[3] and in a 1680 case [4] it was observed that to hold otherwise would not be consistent with the essential nature of a corporate body.

On the other hand, in a day when members were assessable, the corporation could be ordered to require its members to make good its debts under penalty of contempt. This was the procedure called leviation, the subject of a 1671 case.[5]

Until the eighteenth century, however, corporations were not created for business purposes. The closest approximation to the business corporation was the chartered joint stock company, to which limited liability was sometimes granted. The owners of a nonchartered joint stock company were subject to unlimited liability, in the manner of a partnership.

Out of a general movement against joint stock companies, however, a new device arose. The event which brought this about was the infamous South Sea Bubble. The South Sea Company, a chartered joint stock company, took government securities in exchange for its stock in order to assume most of the national debt. Owing to a generally speculative market and to speculation in South Sea Company stock, the price of the stock rose tremendously, and as a result, the Company had to offer less and less of its stock for government securities of a given value. Other companies, despite their differing legal purposes and whether or not they were chartered, saw an opportunity for profit in this market

---

[3] Anon., Y.B. Hy. VI, 80. See C. A. Cooke, *Corporation, Trust and Company* (Manchester: Manchester University Press, 1950), p. 77.

[4] Case of the City of London, 1 Ventr. 351 (1680).

[5] Dr. Salmon v. The Hamborough Company, 1 Ch. Cas. 204 (Am. ed., 1828).

and offered their stock for government securities. In consequence, the price of South Sea stock was depressed. The South Sea Company then obtained the passage of the Bubble Act of 1720,[6] forbidding companies to act without a charter or, if chartered, outside their chartered purposes. The act was meant to protect the South Sea Company's monopoly; its effect, however, was a severe market crash caused by judicial investigations into the activities of competitors. Stocks of all joint stock companies fell in the general decline of stock prices.

The Bubble Act cast a pall over promotions in the form of joint stock companies, and other modes of organization were sought. One approach was to form a partnership but to attempt to permit the assignment of a partner's interest. Another and more successful device was to draw a deed of trust appointing certain individuals trustees (managers) of the fund for the purposes set forth in the instrument. In some cases, provisions were inserted, making the interests of the investors transferable. In addition, some trusts provided that investors were not liable to third parties for the debts of the trusts. This provision was effective, in equity, when third persons, aware of the disclaimer of liability, extended credit to the trust and tried to collect from its investors. This disclaimer is the source of the English use of the word "limited" after a company's name.

Organizations formed for public benefit rather than for private profit were construed to lie outside the intendment of the Bubble Act. During the succeeding century, therefore, to avoid technical infringement of the Bubble Act, some phrase or clause would be inserted to imply a public or beneficial purpose.

The Bubble Act was finally repealed in 1825.[7] The repealing act, however, provided for incorporation with unlimited liability only. The pressure for limited liability and for the ability to act as a joint stock company without a charter continued until 1834, when the Trading Companies Act[8] legally recognized the demand and enabled joint stock companies to sue through their officers. This act and parts of the 1825 act were repealed in 1837, and new provisions were adopted, giving limited liability in amounts varying with each company and not fixed by the amount invested. Still, however, the administering Board of Trade granted privileges only to organizations that could demonstrate some public advantage from their operations.

The Companies Act of 1862[9] (which followed a series of intermediate acts) was the final culmination of this legislative development. It provided for a formal method of incorporation as a joint stock company with or without limited liability. If there were more than twenty members, they had to become a corporation; but if there were fewer than seven members, they had to be a partnership.

---

[6] 6 Geo. I, c. 18.
[7] 6 Geo. IV, c. 91.
[8] 4 & 5 Wm. IV, c. 94.
[9] 25 & 26 Vict., c. 89.

American corporations

American business corporation law does not owe much to English law. Indeed, our law on this subject was developed at an earlier date and was cited as an example by the English to their Parliament; it was a causative factor in modern English law.

After the American Revolution, it was generally understood that limited liability was an attribute of the formally incorporated business organization and that unlimited liability was one of the risks of the joint stock enterprise. Before 1800, about 330 charters of incorporation were granted in America. They were concentrated in New England, and were usually in public-interest ventures such as turnpikes, water companies, and insurance, rather than completely private-profit enterprises. During that time, little bias had grown up against the corporate form of doing business, apparently because dissolution had not been accompanied by injury to creditors.

The doctrine of limited liability (unless the statute creating the corporation provided otherwise) was clearly established in the leading case of *Spear v. Grant*, in 1819.[10] Considerable legislative doubt, however, existed with respect to the propriety of limited liability when applied to purely private-profit institutions. Massachusetts, for instance, adopted and maintained a policy of unlimited liability for such ventures from 1809 to 1830. First the creditor had to exhaust corporate property; and if that did not satisfy his claim, he could levy on the property of individual shareholders. In the case of banks, this era saw the beginning of shareholders' liability for double the amount of their subscriptions, a policy which continued until the 1930's.

Other states had varied legislative policies on the subject of limited liability. After 1816 Connecticut and New Hampshire granted limited liability in all cases and Maine did so after 1823. Rhode Island did not abandon unlimited liability until 1847. New York, on the other hand, was partial to a policy of double liability, while Pennsylvania, except for one year, was an advocate of limited liability. However, since early Pennsylvania legislatures granted corporate charters only for nonindustrial purposes, the question was relatively unimportant.

In general, the adoption of a policy of limited liability awaited some protection of corporate creditors. The courts developed means of preventing premature distribution of corporate assets among the shareholders. The legislatures prohibited the invasion of capital by setting up restrictions on the declaration of dividends. Liability was imposed on shareholders who failed to pay in full for their shares of stock. Experiments with extensive publicity requirements were conducted, in the hope that creditors might be advised of the financial strengths and weaknesses of corporations with which they proposed to deal. These and other financial safeguards were devised in the second quarter of the nineteenth century, in order that the dual aims of creditor protection and limited

---

[10] 16 Mass. 9.

liability could be met. The price of limited liability was respect for the capital stock account.

The classical mode of incorporation was, in this country, by special legislative act. The movement toward general acts started in 1811 in New York. By complying with automatic statutory provisions instead of making separate petitions to the legislature, corporations could be formed in certain businesses if limited to $100,000 in capital and to a corporate life of twenty or fewer years.[11] By 1870 all states had general incorporation acts, but restrictions on corporate purposes and on maximum capitalization were not removed until the beginning of the twentieth century. Until that time, corporate charters were granted only in areas of activity that the legislatures desired to foster.

Modern business corporation law is uniformly based on detailed state statutes. After the Civil War and until the 1930's, many jurisdictions attempted to induce promoters to incorporate in their own states. The advantages offered—including lower taxes and fewer restrictions on management discretion—led to increasing diversity in the corporation laws of the states. In the 1930's, a movement toward uniformity based on sound legal principles began with the Illinois Business Corporation Act of 1933, followed by the Pennsylvania Act of the same year. In 1946, the Committee on Corporate Laws of the American Bar Association published a proposed Model Business Corporation Act which has been adopted by several states. Corporation law, however, is still diverse. Some generalizations can be made, but answers to particular questions still require the investigation of the state law involved.

Partnerships

The partnership is one of the oldest forms of doing business. It is found in ancient Babylonian and Jewish law, in Roman law, and throughout the Middle Ages. Nevertheless, it still creates a great number of conceptual and practical difficulties.

A startling number of questions can arise from the simple statement that a partnership is an association of persons in business for profit. Can a partnership sue or be sued in its own name? Who owns partnership property, the partners or the partnership? Can partnership creditors sue the partners directly for the debts of the partnership? Can partners sell their interests in partnership property? Can partners use partnership property for their individual purposes? Can the act of one partner bind the partnership to liability in contract or to liability in tort? Is an incoming or outgoing partner liable for partnership debts?

Entity and aggregate theories. The basic and underlying question for a legal system to answer is whether it wishes the partnership to be treated as an entity or as an aggregation of individuals. If it is an entity, it can sue and be sued in its own name, own the partnership property, probably

---

[11] Laws of N.Y., 1811, Ch. 67, p. 111.

be solely liable for its debts (although leviation may apply here), and have sole control of its property. Its partners then are agents of the partnership and can bind it to tort or contract liability in accordance with agency principles.

If a partnership is an aggregation of individuals, it cannot sue or be sued in its own name (all the partners must be joined in suit), the partners own partnership property and can sell their interests in it, and they are liable for partnership debts directly.

Neither approach is fully satisfactory. No one would contend that the limited liability of an entity should be an attribute of a partnership, and leviation is too cumbersome a mode of collection by creditors. On the other hand, if a single partner could sell his interest in specific partnership property, as he could under the aggregate theory, he could deprive the partnership of the use of its most essential asset and so frustrate the other partners.

Partnership law was in a state of utmost confusion until the beginning of the twentieth century. As early as 1693, for instance, it was decided that partners owned partnership property as joint tenants.[12] It followed that since each partner owned an undivided interest in each parcel of partnership property, whether real or personal, the creditor of an individual partner could levy on his debtor's interest in partnership property. Although the common-law joint tenant could voluntarily sell his interest in jointly owned property, it was later established that a partner could not voluntarily sell his interest in partnership property. The common-law joint tenancy, in other words, was inadequate to handle the problems created by the partnership. Other problems of equal difficulty included the relative rights of individual and partnership creditors in individual and partnership assets when the partnership was liquidated, whether the executor of a deceased partner had a right to join in winding up a partnership, the rights of partners among themselves during the operation of the business, and the liabilities of incoming partners.

The Uniform Partnership Act. The National Conference of Commissioners on Uniform State Laws began to consider a Uniform Partnership Act in 1902. The first draft was to be based on the entity rather than on the aggregate theory. The entity theory was not only the apparent approach of the law merchant, but it was, hopefully, a solution to the vexing problem of a partner's rights in specific partnership property: by ownership and control of partnership property in the partnership itself, as an entity, creditors of individual partners could not attach it.

Dean William Draper Lewis, of the University of Pennsylvania Law School, assumed responsibility for drafting the act in 1910. He believed that the entity theory would create as many problems as it solved, particularly in the area of liability of partners. The problem was how, under the entity theory, partners were to be made liable for partnership debts. There were three alternatives: first, to treat them as co-principals on all partnership contracts; second, to treat them as sureties; third, to make

---

[12] Heydon v. Heydon, 1 Salk. 392.

them parties to an implied contract to supply the partnership with sufficient money to satisfy the third party.[13]

Each of these courses of action was unsatisfactory. The co-principal theory was a complete fiction. The surety theory would not provide for partners' liability for partnership torts (for which everyone admitted they were and should be liable), and the implied-contract theory would mean a return to the leviation procedure, which had been repudiated in corporation law for almost a century.

These and other questions were answered by taking an intermediate approach. When necessary, the proposed act treated the partnership as an entity or as an aggregation of individuals. The aggregate theory was dominant, however.

Under the act, the partnership can be sued in its own name, which is an application of entity theory. It is provided, however, that unless individual partners are also sued and served with process, only partnership assets can be touched. A like theory was adopted for partnership property, for ownership of the property was placed in the partnership. Therefore, no partner can sell or encumber it, and it is not subject to the claims of the creditors of individual partners. The interest of the partners is solely in the partnership business, not in its assets. In order to give a creditor of an individual partner some recourse against the debtor partner's interest in the partnership, the creditor can obtain a court order turning over his debtor's share of partnership profits to him until he is paid off or until the partnership comes to its natural termination, at which time he can attach the debtor's interest in partnership property directly.

The aggregate theory was recognized by providing that partners may be sued directly for partnership contract debts and that they are directly liable for partnership torts, reserving to the partners a right of contribution for payments in excess of their shares for their co-partners.

The Uniform Partnership Act has been adopted by nearly two-thirds of the states and has profoundly influenced the course of the law. The act illustrates the difficulty of relying on the direct application of common-law doctrines to solve business problems. On the other hand, it demonstrates the fact that judicious building on the foundation of the common law, rejecting that which is obsolete or inapplicable, changing that which is malleable, and developing new principles where required can foster sound legal growth and consolidation. No legal system can do more, and no legal system should do less.

---

[13] W. D. Lewis, "The Uniform Partnership Act—A Reply to Mr. Crane's Criticism," 29 *Harv. L. Rev* 158, 165-66 (1915).

Suggested readings

General legal works

The most complete work on English legal history is the thirteen volume *A History of English Law* by W. S. Holdsworth. It was published between the years 1903 and 1952, the last volume appearing posthumously. There are several editions of this history.

Pollock and Maitland, *The History of English Law before the Time of Edward I* (2 vols., 2nd ed., 1898) is a true classic. It is not only highly authoritative, but also worthy of a place in literature.

Two current English books should be considered together. Both Plucknett, *A Concise History of the Common Law* (5th ed., 1956) and Potter, *Historical Introduction to English Law and Its Institutions* (4th ed. by A. K. R. Kiralfy, 1958) are standard texts. Both are well documented and highly authoritative. Potter is somewhat more detailed than Plucknett, but the latter is easier and more enjoyable reading, because of its simpler form of organization and more facile writing. Plucknett has had an excellent reception in this country.

Two American texts are Radin, *Handbook of Anglo-American Legal History* (1936) and Walsh, *A History of Anglo-American Law* (2nd ed., 1932).

Jenks, *A Short History of English Law* (4th ed., 1928) is a survey. It is a well-written general treatment, not intended as a reference volume.

A comprehensive treatment of American legal history has yet to be written. Our fifty separate states and nine geographical regions create complexities of great magnitude. The gaps in Colonial records and their diverse repositories further complicate the task.

Topical references

For those interested in further exploration of particular topics, the following secondary sources are mentioned:

Part I—The Background of the Law

BOOKS: Abraham, *The Judicial Process* (1962), particularly Chap. 6 on foreign legal training. Allen, *Law in the Making* (5th ed., 1951), Chap. 5 on equity. Cam, *Law-Finders and Law-Makers in Medieval England* (1963). Goebel, ed., *Cases and Materials on the Development of Legal Institutions* (1946). Harno, *Legal Education in the United States* (1953). Haskins, G. L.,

Law and Authority in Early Massachusetts (1960). Howe, *Readings in American Legal History* (1949). Loyd, *The Early Courts of Pennsylvania* (1910). MacKenzie, *The English Parliament* (1951). Maitland, *Domesday Book and Beyond* (1897). Mayers, *The Machinery of Justice* (in this series). Warren, *A History of the American Bar* (1911).

ARTICLES: Adams, "Origin of English Equity," 16 *Col. L. Rev.* 87 (1916). Chitwood, "Justice in Colonial Virginia," *Johns Hopkins Univ. Studies,* Series 23, Nos. 7, 8 (1905). Keigwin, "The Origin of Equity," 18 *Geo. L. J.* 15, 92, 215, 299 (1929-1930); 19 *Geo. L. J.* 48, 165 (1930-1931). Pope, "The English Common Law in the United States," 24 *Harv. L. Rev.* 6 (1910). Pound, "The Development of American Law and Its Deviation from English Law," 67 *L. Q. Rev.* 49 (1951). Reinsch, "The English Common Law in the American Colonies," 1 *Select Essays in Anglo-American Legal History* 367 (1907). Whitney, "Government of the Colony of South Carolina," *Johns Hopkins Univ. Studies,* Series 13, Nos. 1, 2 (1895). Zane, "The Five Ages of the Bench and Bar in England," 1 *Select Essays in Anglo-American Legal History* 625, (1907).

Part II—Sources of Law

BOOKS Allen, *Law in the Making* (5th ed., 1951), Chaps. 5 and 6. 3 Pound, *Jurisprudence* (1959), Chap. 19.

ARTICLES: Elias, "Colonial Courts and the Doctrine of Judicial Precedent," 18 *Mod. L. Rev.* 356 (1955). Kempin, "Precedent and *Stare Decisis:* The Critical Years, 1800-1850," 3 *Am. J. Legal Hist.* 28 (1959). Milner, "Restatement: The Failure of a Legal Experiment," 20 *U. Pitt. L. Rev.* 795 (1959). Pegues, "The Medieval Origins of Modern Law Reporting," 38 *Cornell L. Q.* 491 (1953). Riesenfeld, "Law-Making and Legislative Precedent in American Legal History," 33 *Minn. L. Rev.* 103 (1949).

Part III—The Common Law in Action

BOOKS: Digby, *An Introduction to the History of the Law of Real Property* (1875). Moynihan, *A Preliminary Survey of the Law of Real Property* (1940), particularly Chaps. 1, 2, and 3.

ARTICLES: Ames, "The History of Assumpsit," 3 *Harv. L. Rev.* 1, 53, 377 (1888), also found in 3 *Select Essays in Anglo-American Legal History* 259 (1909). Holdsworth, "The Modern History of the Doctrine of Consideration," 2 *B.U.L. Rev.* 87, 174 (1922), also found in *Selected Readings on the Law of Contracts* 61 (1931). Landon, "The Action on the Case and the Statute of Westminster II," 52 *L. Q. Rev.* 68 (1936). Pollock, "Contracts in Early English Law," 6 *Harv. L. Rev.* 389 (1893), also found in *Selected Readings on the Law of Contracts* 10 (1931). Reppy, "History of the Law of Wills and Testaments in England," 16 *Geo. L. J.* 194 (1928). Salmond, "The History of Contract," 3 *L. Q. Rev.* 166 (1887), also found in 3 *Select Essays in Anglo-American Legal History* 320 (1909). Winfield, "The Myth of Absolute Liability," 42 *L. Q. Rev.* 37 (1926). Winfield, "The History of Negligence in the Law of Torts," 42 *L. Q. Rev.* 184 (1926). Winfield and Goodhart, "Trespass and Negligence," 49 *L. Q. Rev.* 359 (1933).

Part IV—The Common Law "Codified"

BOOKS: Davis, *Eighteenth Century Business Corporations in the United States* (1917). Dodd, *American Business Corporations Until 1860* (1954). Cooke, *Corporation, Trust and Company* (1950). Holden, *The History of Negotiable Instruments in English Law* (1955).

ARTICLES: Drake, "Partnership Entity and Tenancy in Partnership: The Struggle for a Definition," 15 *Mich. L. Rev.* 609 (1917). Hunt, "The Joint-Stock Company in England, 1800-1825," 43 *J. Pol. Econ.* 1 (1935). Kerr, "The Origin and Development of the Law Merchant," 15 *Va. L. Rev.* 350 (1929). Lewis, "The Uniform Partnership Act—A Reply to Mr. Crane's Criticism," 29 *Harv. L. Rev.* 158, 291 (1915-1916). Livermore, "Unlimited Liability in Early American Corporations," 43 *J. Pol. Econ.* 674 (1935). Williston, "History of the Law of Business Corporations Before 1800," 2 *Harv. L. Rev.* 105 (1888).

General background

The following books may prove helpful in providing background material.

Buckland and McNair, *Roman Law and Common Law* (2nd ed., 1952). Davis, *England under the Normans and Angevins, 1066-1272* (1937). Dicey, *Law and Public Opinion in England during the Nineteenth Century* (1905). Friedmann, *Law and Social Change in Contemporary Britain* (1951). Maine, *Ancient Law* (1861). Pound, *The Spirit of the Common Law* (1921). Pound and Plucknett, *Readings on the History and System of the Common Law* (1927). Round, *Feudal England* (1895). Smith, *A Constitutional and Legal History of England* (1955). F. M. Stenton, *Anglo-Saxon England* (1943). Wigmore, *A Panorama of the World's Legal System* (1 vol. ed., 1936).

Index

ACKNOWLEDGMENTS

My primary debt is owed to the writers who, over the past eighty years, have labored among the old cases and statutes, have discovered hidden sources, and have spun theories to explain the growth of our law. The names of the pioneers, W. S. Holdsworth and F. W. Maitland, and of the later scholars, Helen Cam, Julius Goebel, Mark deWolfe Howe, T. F. T. Plucknett, and Harold Potter, are synonymous with legal history; one cannot even enter its vestibule without their assistance. To have cited these and other eminent scholars each time they were relied on would have overburdened this small book. Therefore this omnibus acknowledgment is due. Special thanks are extended to Professor George L. Haskins, of the University of Pennsylvania Law School, for his helpful comments and criticisms at an early stage in the development of this book.

Frederick G. Kempin, Jr.